W^{and the}ORD
came with
POWER

WORD
and the
came with
POWER

JOANNE SHETLER
WITH PATRICIA PURVIS

Wycliffe
Partners in Bible Translation
Orlando, Florida
1-800-WYCLIFFE • www.wycliffe.org

Visit Wycliffe's Web site at www.wycliffe.org

And The Word Came With Power
Copyright © 1992, 2000 and 2002 by Wycliffe Bible Translators, Inc.
P.O. Box 628200
Orlando, Florida 32862-8200

First Printing 1992 by Multnomah Press
Second Printing 2000 by Wycliffe Bible Translators, Inc.
Third Printing 2002 by Wycliffe Bible Translators, Inc.

Cover design by Jewel Fink and Justin Wills

Unless otherwise indicated, all Scripture references are from the Holy
Bible: New International Version, copyright © 1973, 1978, 1984 by the
International Bible Society. Used by permission of Zondervan Bible
Publishers.

Library of Congress Cataloging-in-Publication Data
    Shetler, Joanne.
    And the word came with power: how God met and changed a
people forever/Joanne Shetler with Patricia Purvis.
        p. cm.
    ISBN 0-938978-31-4.
    Balangao (Philippine people)—Missions. 2. Shetler, Joanne.
I. Purvis, Patricia A. II. Title
BV3380.S54 1991
266'.0089'9921—dc20

                          91-38338
                            CIP

Printed in the United States of America

Contents

Acknowledgments

Translating a New Testament is a long, hard job. I didn't translate the Balangao New Testament by myself. The men and women mentioned in this book are only a representative few of the many people who were indispensable to the work. They wrote this story with their lives.

I couldn't have done the translation without my partners: Anne Fetzer Hopkins, Edie Murdock, Janet Pack Persons, Marjorie Cook, Mary Jo Brett, Barbara Williams Harris and Robyn Terrey. The rest of the team in the Philippines was also essential: pilots, radio operators and technicians, librarians, the computer people—technicians, programmers and keyboarders—the printing arts department, maintenance men, administrators, buyers, pray-ers, friends—the list goes on.

My church families back in the United States were the broad roots supporting the spreading tree of God's work in Balangao. Without their teaching, I never would have gone to the Philippines; without their friendship, I never could have stayed there; without their gifts, I never would have eaten; and without their prayers, we never would have seen spiritual fruit.

And then there is Patricia Purvis who said yes when I asked her to shape my memories into this book. The writing of the book was a family affair. Her husband Norm encouraged her to tackle the task that "couldn't be done" in the time allotted. Then he and their three sons, Matthew,

Michael and Kevin, fondly tolerated her preoccupation with the book, prayed for her, encouraged her, and were enthusiastic every time she read the manuscript out loud to them.

Books don't happen without editors. Liz Heaney was one of our Balangao prayer partners, a vital part of the team back in 1981 and 1982 when she was teaching at Faith Academy in Manila. Now at Multnomah Press, she has skillfully edited the whole story with keen insight and encouragement to all of us.

And then there's my Balangao family and friends. What a rich treasure! I thought I had come to give to them, but they started giving to me before I had a chance to learn even one word of their language.

They carried my water, planted my rice, invited me to dinner, taught me their customs and language, forgave me when I offended them, corrected me when I spoke Balangao "like a water buffalo," and ably assisted me in translating the New Testament. Sometimes they believed the truth from the Word of God when I was hesitant to do the same.

From them, I gained much more than I gave. It was the privilege of my life to live and work with these fine people and to bring them God's Word and watch it change their lives.

A Beginning Word

And the Word Came with Power is really a love story. From the beginning God loved the Balangao people, proud headhunters who lived on the magnificent rice terraces of the Philippines. And he loved me, a shy farm girl from California who was inclined to trust God and dream big dreams.

God set in motion events in our worlds and in our hearts that brought us together. And as I translated the Word of God into the Balangao language, the Balangaos and I became embroiled in a spiritual battle that changed our worlds forever.

God repeatedly invited us to risk trusting him and his Word. He took each of us as we were, with our limited understanding of ourselves and our world. As we trusted God, he drew us closer to himself and we learned more about his power and love. I've written these pages so that you might stand along with us in praise and wonder at the overwhelming love of God and his relentless pursuit of us.

Jo Shetler

THE PHILIPPINES

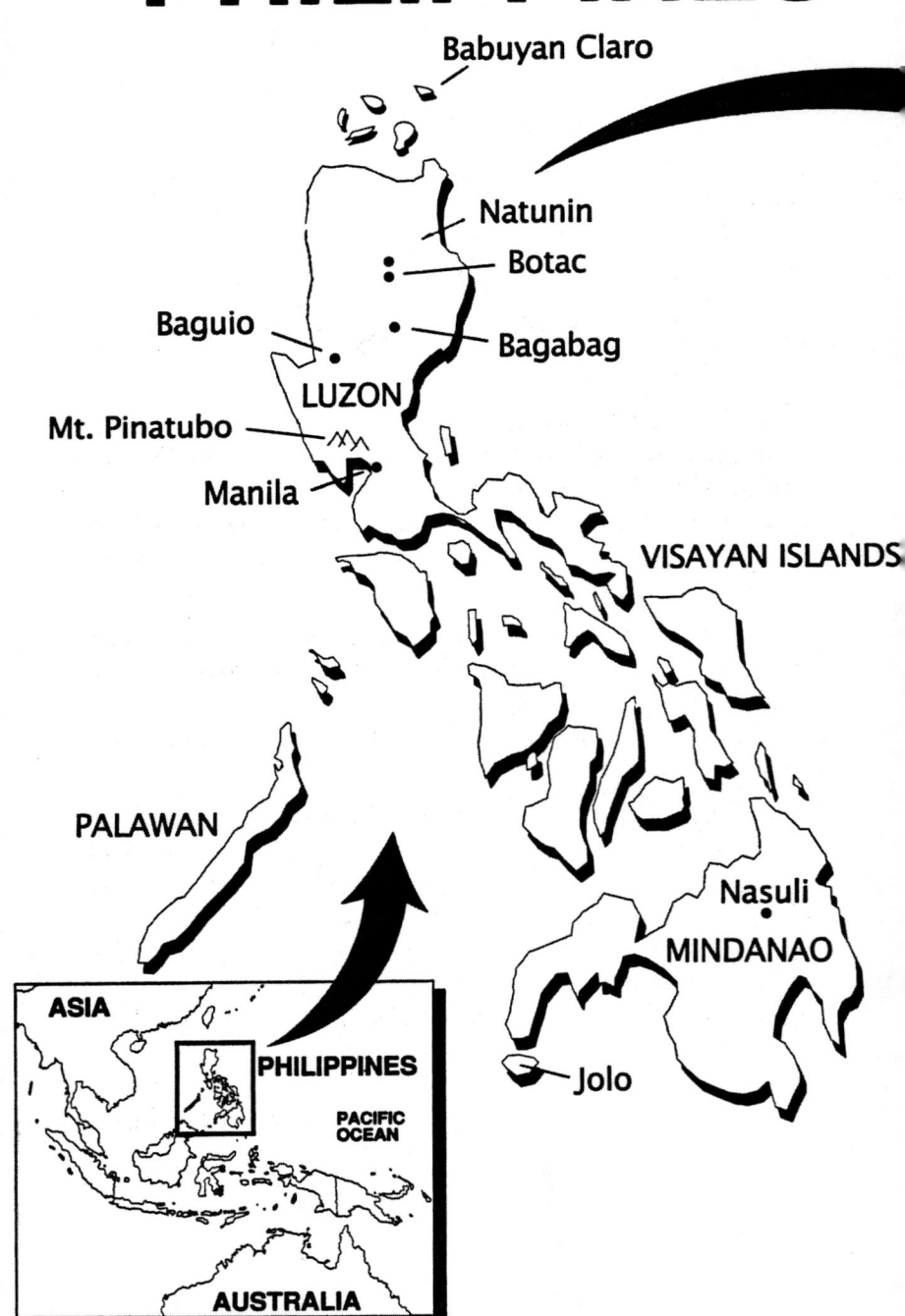

Babuyan Claro

Natunin

Botac

Baguio

Bagabag

LUZON

Mt. Pinatubo

Manila

VISAYAN ISLANDS

PALAWAN

Nasuli

MINDANAO

ASIA

PHILIPPINES

PACIFIC
OCEAN

Jolo

AUSTRALIA

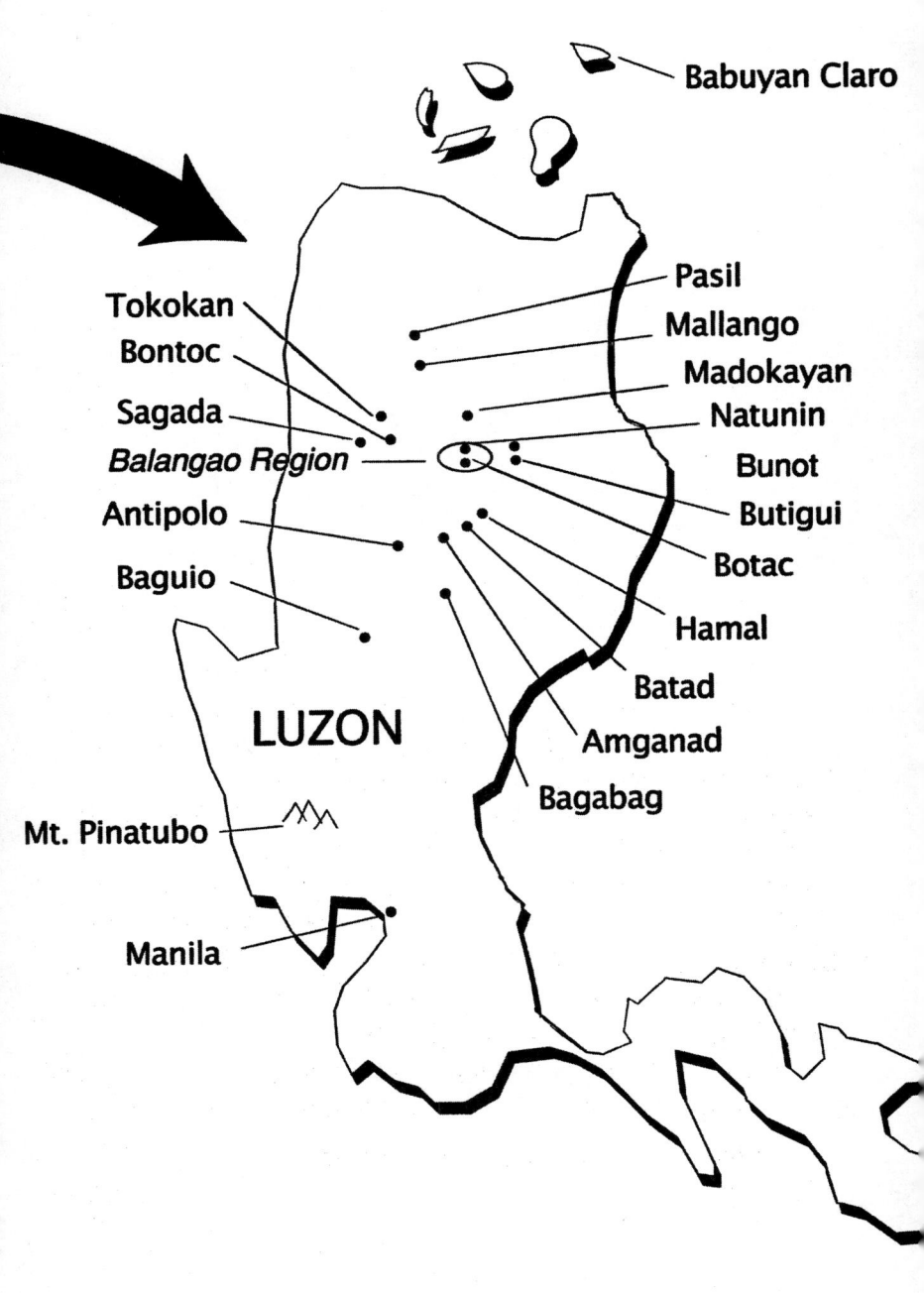

Babuyan Claro

Pasil
Mallango
Madokayan
Tokokan
Bontoc
Natunin
Sagada
Balangao Region
Bunot
Butigui
Antipolo
Botac
Baguio
Hamal

LUZON

Batad
Amganad
Bagabag

Mt. Pinatubo

Manila

1
Don't Let Her Die!

I waved excitedly out the window of the Jolly Green Giant helicopter as we approached a small, flattened knoll—the basketball court—in our little mountain town in the Philippines. The Balangao people gathered below waved back and shouted up at us. They couldn't wait to unload the tons of cement, glass, and nails we were carrying to build their new hospital.

Beside me, young Dr. Robespierre Lim ran back and forth from window to window, waving and calling to people. Robbie's dream was finally coming true—a hospital in Balangao. Now my medical work would be lessened and I could concentrate on translating the New Testament.

We started our descent. Funny...it didn't seem quite the right place. Suddenly, the fronds of a betel nut palm flew past my window. I gasped. *We've hit a tree. We're going to crash!*

Later, as consciousness returned, I heard muted shouts of my Balangao name, "Juami!" and, "Fire! Fire! Run!" I summoned my strength and strained to break loose and escape from the burning helicopter. But all I could move were two fingers of my left hand. I was wedged in like a driven nail.

I started to panic. *Think about something—anything. How can my right arm be twisted up like that when my hand is cupped over my mouth and nose?* I focused on that impossible contortion and kept swallowing dry, dusty cement powder, trying to clear the airways for each breath.

Save your energy. Keep recycling that air. How long does it take to burn to death? The thoughts came with odd detachment.

God, I can't die yet!

I had no idea what was happening outside: After the crash, the pilots had jumped out to a horrible sight—fuel spewed out from a big gash in the craft and flames leapt from the remains of the rotor blades. They yelled to the Balangaos standing stunned beside the wreckage, "Run! It's going to explode!"

But when the Balangaos heard Doming, Dr. Lim, and I were trapped inside, they all turned in mid-flight, grabbed aluminum rice pots, plastic buckets and basins, anything they could find in a hurry, and started throwing mud and water from the rice fields on the burning aircraft. In a matter of minutes they put out the fires.

But all I knew was that I was trying not to panic. I assessed my medical situation. *No broken bones, but my head is jammed hard to one side and pinned tight—another half-inch and my neck would have been broken.*

How long can I keep breathing only a handful of air? God, don't let me suffocate! I've got to finish this translation.

Suddenly I realized, *Someone's up there on top of me!* I muffled out a cry for help. The Balangaos say it sounded like a meow from within the wreckage and they started digging frantically, tearing away with their hands at shattered glass, broken crates of nails, torn sacks of cement, and the rubble of broken helicopter gear.

Someone grabbed my feet and tried to pull me upward. I'd been found! I realized I was lying head down, feet up. "Don't just pull my feet," I gasped. "Make me an airway! I can't breathe!"

A bag of cement was yanked away from my chest, allowing a draft of air to sweep in. It was delicious. I gulped it in as the Balangaos pulled and pulled. Finally, I squirmed loose.

Frightened Balangaos carried me down the trail to a nearby building and laid me on the rough, wooden floor of a large room. Blood from the gashes in my head mixed with the thick layer of cement powder which coated my body. The blood scared the Balangaos.

If only I could get my breath and open my eyes—maybe the others need help. I didn't realize my ribs were broken and one lung had collapsed. My eyes had been open while I was unconscious and were filled with powdered cement. The caustic lime in the cement ate into the tissues of my eyes. They felt like they were on fire.

Trying to sound authoritative, I slowly gave instructions: "You must wash my eyes out. Get a pitcher of water, hold my eyes open, and pour the water in. Do it again and again."

But I couldn't even turn my head so they could pour the water in; I couldn't move my swollen neck. I told them, "Turn my head for me by pulling on my hair…pour water…."

The water felt like live coals pressing against my eyeballs. I insisted in a hoarse whisper, "Continue." When the pain literally took my breath away, they stopped. I breathed, and then I whispered again, urgently, "Keep pouring the water in!"

God, I can't go blind—I won't be able to finish this translation if I'm blind.

"It's OK if it hurts, keep pouring the water in!"

They gently pried my eyes open and washed them, hour after hour. It was a night of torture.

Meanwhile, some teenagers had raced nearly an hour down the mountain to our tiny village of Botac with the news. Ama, my gray-haired, adopted Balangao father, was splitting firewood when he heard the shrieks: "The helicopter crashed! The doctor's dead. Juami and Doming are crushed!" Ama's hand axe froze in mid-air. His oldest son,

Doming, and his American daughter, Juami—both in a helicopter? Crushed?

He dropped his axe and took off running along the narrow trails on top of the rice terrace dikes. As he leapt up steep stone steps jutting out of rock walls, he cried out, "Oh, God, what happened to Job has happened to me—all my children are lost in a single night!" The shock had driven his other five children from his mind.

Tekla, who had become a close sister to me, had heard the news at the same time. She was sitting on the floor of her thatched-roofed house eating dinner with the smaller children. As soon as she heard, she flew down her short bamboo ladder, leaving her children unattended and bowls of food on the floor. Racing up the trail, she overtook Ama. Up, up the mountain, her bare feet pounded the dirt and rocks. Memories of countless warnings against translating the Scriptures flooded her memory: "God will punish you for touching the untouchable, for polluting the holy! God will punish you!" Was it true? Had they desecrated the holy Word of God?

Before the last steep ascent, Tekla prayed, "Oh, holy God, it's up to you. Maybe those people are right and we have desecrated your holy Word by putting it into our lowly language. And if so, then we accept our punishment and Juami will die. But God, if that's not true, and if you really do want your Word in our language, then let her live—don't let her die. But God, I need a sign—I need to know…if I call out 'Juami' and she answers back, 'Tekla,' then I'll know she will live."

The room I was in was packed with people. They crowded around me with their last gift—their presence when I died. Through the commotion, I heard Tekla burst into the room, "Juami! Juami!"

"Tekla, Tekla, it's OK. I'll be OK." My voice was weak; I couldn't get enough air to push it out.

Tekla turned to the quietly weeping crowd and said, "She'll live! She'll live!"

Spurning her words, they looked down at me, a ghostly pile of bloodied cement and grotesquely bulging eyes. "Can't you see she's already dead—just her breath is left."

"God will keep her alive," Tekla said. "She'll be all right, I know." And Tekla took over for the night.

"Tell us what to do—just tell us what to do," she coaxed me.

I could tell I was going into shock. "Blankets…coffee…." Tekla sent for blankets and lots of strong, hot coffee.

Why can't I get my breath?

Tekla sent some children down the mountain to my house for clean clothes. She had to cut off my heavy, stiff dress; then she gently washed me, talking to me quietly and calling to others for clean water, towels, and more coffee. Another friend sutured the long gashes in my head. I didn't feel the needle; I didn't even feel the broken ribs or the jagged edges of my collarbone. Nothing could compete with the excruciating pain of my eyes.

Whispered snatches of conversation had assured me that my Balangao brother Doming was OK and so were all the pilots and crew. But no one had mentioned Robbie. I knew he must be in bad shape. *If only I could help him.* Toward morning a priest knelt beside me, and brokenly told me they'd kept Robbie alive until midnight.

I mourned briefly, but the pain in my eyes consumed my focus. I remembered some anesthetic eye ointment in my medicine cabinet and had Tekla send someone down the mountain for it.

It didn't help.

Someone brought Robbie's doctor bag which I knew contained some Demerol. In short, labored sentences, I explained how to inject some into me. The pain never wavered, but the medicine did make me vomit a mountain of cement, slushy with coffee.

The night was long, the pain intense. But something else was going on. Something new for Balangaos. One by one, throughout the night, Balangao Christians worked their way through the throng, touched my hand, and prayed. I'll never forget their prayers: "God, don't let her die, the Book's not done yet. Just let her live; the Book's not done yet."

For months I had longed for the Balangao Christians to get past their short, perfunctory prayers. I'd often awakened in the middle of the night, begging God to teach them to pray. Three months earlier I'd written home asking friends to pray:

"The believers need to learn to pray with intensity. They need to understand that their own powers are useless, even in doing 'godly' things, and that only what God performs will be real in people's lives…If there is a longing in my heart, it is that God would make these Balangaos a people of effective, powerful prayer."

Desperate, I had carefully told God, "I don't care what you have to do; make these people pray!"

That night, as I lay on the floor, more dead than alive, the Balangaos were praying—really praying. One after another, they prayed the same prayer, "Don't let her die, the Book's not done yet."

It was the worst and best night of my life all wrapped up in one. The worst pain I'd ever known was eclipsed by moments of indescribable awe over their prayers. Only God could weave such extremes.

2

I Let My Dream Die!

❖⟨❈⟩❖

I grew up on a farm in Southern California.

Early in the morning, before anyone else was awake, I used to call our collie, Laddie, and we'd saunter over the hills and down through gullies of our 1,000-acre farm and watch the sun come up. Soft, lacy Spanish moss dripping from the oak trees looked other-worldly in morning's first light, and the yellow of buttercups was richer then.

I'd dream about the house I'd have some day: a big, beautiful farmhouse with a white fence. Cows would graze on the rolling hills surrounding it. Best of all, my house would be crowded with happy people. Occasionally in my dream, I'd leave my house and friends and go to the hospital where I worked as a nurse, like my mom. To me, it was the perfect life.

As I snapped back to reality, I'd dash back home in time to cook breakfast for the family and help with chores before school.

One day when I was seven, Dad and I were out in the field pulling weeds. He straightened up and told me to go back and bring the pickup over to him. I sputtered, "But... but...I don't know how to drive."

Dad was unimpressed. My brothers had been driving by age seven. Dad believed two things: "You don't have to know how, you just have to do it," and "You can do anything you want to—you just have to work hard to do it." Impossibilities? There were no such things. He didn't quit and he wouldn't let us quit. Ever.

So, trembling, I ran over to the truck, my heart in my throat. Somehow I got it started and it lurched toward Dad. I only did it because he told me to. From an early age, I'd learned you don't argue with authority.

Dad showed us love the best way he knew—by preparing us to meet and overcome the challenges of life. That legacy has been invaluable to me.

I respected my dad, but I was also a bit afraid of him. And this aspect was also part of his legacy. When Dad said "Jump," I'd ask, "How high?" Automatically I transferred these feelings to God.

But I've learned something about God that transformed my fear into a reverential awe of him: *God uses absolutely everything.* He'll even take what seems like cow manure and turn it into his useful material. He'll make it fertilizer for his glory—but only if we give it to him. If we harbor it, the pile just stinks. It's OK to have hard spots in your life; everybody has them, I'm convinced. But the only way to access God's gifts is to work through those hard spots.

I always felt awkward and out of place at school. Here I was, this tall farm girl in feed-sack dresses with stick-straight hair. My brothers and I always had to take the school bus home right after school. There were cows to milk, chickens to feed, weeds to hoe, and wood to carry. When I was with the kids from town, looking so neat in their store-bought clothes, I never knew how to act.

But at age eleven I knew what to do when I heard that God offered forgiveness for sins and eternal life if I just asked him for it. My hand shot up when the Bible club teacher asked who wanted to accept Christ as their Savior. That was the best news I'd ever heard of—it was like discovering gold.

My brothers and I began attending Bible club when our pastor offered to drive us all the way home afterward. During those rides home he showed us what God was like. Pastor Brown liked us! He laughed, he joked, and he talked about God's Word.

Because I respected authority, it wasn't difficult to believe God's Word. But I was troubled by the command to go out into all the world to share the Good News and to teach people about God. One Sunday a missionary came to our church; he said that 90 percent of the "go-ers," "tellers," and "makers-of-disciples" were concentrating on only 10 percent of the world's population.

I sat up straight in my seat. That left the other 10 percent of the "go-ers," "tellers," and "makers-of-disciples" to somehow reach 90 percent of the world. His logic left me weak, but it made sense. I was going to have to be a missionary—whatever that meant.

Later, at summer camp, a missionary speaker told us that if we were planning to be missionaries we'd better start praying now for the people to whom God would send us one day. That made sense, too. Daily I prayed, "Lord, prepare those people so they'll be ready for the Gospel, so they'll believe."

But I had many questions: What do missionaries actually do? How do they know when they've finished? What could I do that would last forever? What if the only thing the people ever learn about God is what I tell them? I'd listen as missionaries talked, but I couldn't see myself in such a role. I felt inadequate for the task.

One day I realized, "Going into all the world to preach the Gospel" means I'll have to live in a jungle! As far as I knew, everything outside of America was a jungle. As a high schooler, I'd hardly been out of San Luis Obispo County.

I argued with God. *What about my dream farmhouse, the rolling hills, the nursing? What have I gotten myself into?* I fought. I told him over and over, "You must have the wrong person—I can't do this. I don't even know what a missionary is." But God seemed as unimpressed as my father had been when I told him I couldn't drive the pickup. God wouldn't accept my inadequacies as an excuse.

After months of struggle, I gave in and finally told God, "OK, I'll do it. I'll do it, even if I hate it."

I said goodbye to my farmhouse, my career, my family—everything I'd wanted. I let my dream die.

3
An Isolated Sand Bar

A s I let go of my dreams, my excitement about being a
missionary started to grow. My pastor told me I could
find out what a missionary did if I went to a Christian college, so I enrolled in the Christian Education program at
Biola College.

One night after classes a friend and I were talking in
Biola's basement coffee shop. She paused and looked
down into her cup. Then she looked up and dropped a
bomb on me: "Joanne, do you realize that people think
you're stuck-up?"

"What? *Me?* I just don't know what to say to people!"

"I know that," she said. "But most people don't understand why you don't talk to them. They think you don't like

them." Then she took me under her wing and gave me some hints: "Just smile and 'play ball.' When someone throws you the conversational ball, throw it back to them. Enter into the situation and don't worry so much about yourself or how you come across. Make the other person feel comfortable."

I started to experiment with what she told me, and little by little I could talk to others. The shyness never went away, but I began to look at life through eyes aimed outward instead of inward. I began to see things from other people's perspectives.

When I graduated from college I had a box crammed with material from just about every mission in the world, and only a vague idea about what a missionary really did. I was still scared to death that what I told a group of people about God might be all they would ever know about him.

I was wondering what to do next when I heard about a summer course at the University of Oklahoma where they taught people how to learn foreign languages. I didn't particularly like languages, but I knew I'd have to learn another language when I was a missionary. I figured this course might help. So I studied linguistic analysis with the Summer Institute of Linguistics.

Bible translation is so logical. That attracted me…I figured a person who could easily drift off into dreams needed to be anchored by logic. Also, since the Bible is the most important book in the world, it follows that it should be translated for people who've never had it in their own language.

Slowly, I began to realize that this was a definable job. I'd know when I started and I'd know when I finished. If I gave people God's Word in their own language, God himself could speak to them directly, and I wouldn't be responsible for giving limited information.

And here was a work that would last forever. Bells rang and lights flashed. At last I knew the thing for which God had made me: Bible translation.

I joined Wycliffe Bible Translators that summer. Several months later, machete in handbag and duffel bag over my shoulder, I headed for Wycliffe's jungle camp training in southern Mexico. Anne Fetzer, a fellow student from the summer course, was there, too. She had an aura about her. Attractive, bright, friendly, and adventuresome, she was also a lady. Anne enjoyed everyone immensely; she knew everyone and everyone knew her. I was excited—and scared—when the staff assigned the two of us to be partners for the duration of jungle camp. From then on, everything was a lark. Even the hard things.

Our first stretching assignment was to build a shelter to live in for six weeks. But we figured we could hang our jungle hammocks under the stars a little longer and delay a bit to complete another project. We pulled out our machetes, and right next to where our shelter would be we cleared away brush and fashioned an outdoor cathedral. After all, first things first.

We had so much fun building our own shelter that we didn't mind the work. We felled trees, chopped cane, dug post holes, tied things together with vines and bark, and hung our jungle hammocks. We carried endless buckets of mud to fashion a stove. Then we fanned and blew and fanned and blew to get a fire going inside it. All this we called home.

Anne and I were in training and supposedly surviving on the limited goods we had carried in, plus what we could forage from the jungle. When our coffee ran out after a few weeks, Anne pointed out that there were coffee trees in the jungle and people who harvested the beans. Besides, what would she and I do without coffee at night around the fire? She invited a couple of the young single men for dinner and suggested they buy some coffee from the Indians who lived in the area. When we ran out of food, we struck up a deal with two women nearby whose mud stove never worked right: If they'd provide the food, we'd cook it.

Anne's sense of freedom and acceptance released in me the adventure and creativity that had been trapped by my lack of confidence. Together we could cope with any challenge, have fun, and include others at the same time. Anne wasn't afraid of anything; and with her out in front, neither was I.

But as jungle camp ended and I still didn't have a long-term partner for Bible translation, I was afraid to ask Anne to be my partner. Why would someone like Anne want a partner like me?

And besides, when Anne and I would sit by the fire at night and talk for hours over cups of coffee, one name kept coming up over and over again: Tommy Hopkins. She and Tommy had grown up together. Friends, just friends, she insisted, from way back. Some of the single men at jungle camp were interested in Anne and she liked them, but she'd always sigh and wonder why she couldn't get seriously interested in any of them.

"I know," I'd say, "it's because you're in love with Tommy Hopkins."

"Oh, I am not. I just love him like a brother and that's all," she'd always answer. But I knew better.

After jungle camp I boarded a bus and went to live for a few weeks in a small village with a translator before my second set of summer courses with Wycliffe.

That first experience of living in a village was a disaster. I returned home sick with disappointment about the experience and about myself. If this was missionary work, I was going back to the farm. But because of my upbringing, I couldn't let myself quit. Yet I was petrified to consider a permanent assignment. I couldn't choose where to work; I didn't have a partner; I couldn't make any decisions.

Why can't I trust God? Why am I so afraid?

When it was my turn to talk with Wycliffe about my future assignment, I crumpled into tears. I was certain Wycliffe wouldn't allow me to remain a member when I couldn't trust God for the unknown. But instead of dismissing me, Wycliffe suggested a temporary assignment, a year in Guatemala. I was elated. They saw my weaknesses, but they still wanted me.

Then my gratefulness evaporated. *What if I can't do this?* But in spite of my fears, I decided to try again. I went to Guatemala for a year.

Hiking over the mountains of Guatemala, I fell in love with its beauty and its people. Every village had its own unique, colorful costume: red, white, and blue here; hand-woven white trousers with purple stripes there. Little boys dressed just like their granddaddies. Every village was quaint. This was an adventure land that could have come right out of my childhood book of fairy tales.

I was standing on a hill looking at a magnificent lake, when someone told me the lake was really a volcanic crater. An ancient world of Mayan ruins was still standing below its calm, cool waters. I wanted to see that underwater city; it captured my imagination.

Why, I could do Bible translation here. I'll get a partner, and we'll live with these people…we'll eat hot, fresh tortillas…we'll learn to dive down to the bottom of the lake and discuss those ancient ruins. This is it! And that day, a new dream was born.

Meanwhile, I developed my policy on dealing with new situations: wait two weeks before evaluating the living conditions. If I dwelled on the difficulties at first, I'd be depressed. However, after two weeks I had figured out how to get drinking water, where to bathe, what to use for light at night, and even how to create something workable for a bathroom.

While in Guatemala, I also finally began to understand what it meant to be a missionary. I lived with translators,

Ken and Bobbie Williams, who were excellent role models. Living with them was like sitting in the front seat and watching Dad drive the car. The Williamses were living video footage of how to be a missionary.

They had beautiful relationships with the Chuj people, the church, and their own daughters. Ken spent hours each day explaining Scripture, in what others would call "discipling." *So Bible translation makes disciples*, I thought. I watched as Ken and Bobbie made good friends with the mothers who brought in their children with sores and cuts and other medical needs. I learned the wonders of worm medicine: a single dose could produce sixty pencil-long worms—the Chuj counted them—from a two-year-old child. I was beginning to see how to do it, how to be a missionary.

Just before I returned to the States, I got a letter from Anne telling me she was ready for an assignment and asking me if I still needed a partner. I wrote her right back, "Yes! And I have just the place for us here in Guatemala!" I described everything to her.

She answered my letter with terrible news: She'd already been assigned to the field of greatest need—the Philippines. *The Philippines?* I thought. *That isolated sand bar with a coconut tree? That flat, hot place?*

For a month, I struggled and prayed and fought with God. *How can I decide?* I could have a like-minded, congenial friend for a partner and live on a hot, sandy island or I could work in the mountains of Guatemala—but at the risk of an unknown partner. The trouble was, I wanted both the partner and the place.

But there was never any choice. Of course I'd go with Anne; like-mindedness is so important. I let another dream die.

4

What Have We Gotten Ourselves Into?

Anne and I stepped off the *S.S. Michigan* and onto Philippine soil on February 20, 1962. Colleagues met us at the dock and drove us home through the port areas and slums. I'd never seen any place like the inner city of Manila. My heart ached as I saw pitiful, thin children wandering the streets alone and the make-do arrangements of tin and wood for houses. Peering out the van window, I swallowed hard.

But we didn't waste time on second thoughts. On the way to the guest house, we asked about possible places to live and start a translation. Wycliffe, we were told, had just finished surveying the languages up north and had learned that a group of people living a two-days' hike beyond the

33

end of the road needed a Bible translation. Help! We weren't interested in anything that remote.

In fact, we'd heard about a beautiful, spring-fed swimming hole down at the southern Wycliffe center in Nasuli. "Aren't there any people near there who need a translation?" we asked hopefully. But there were none.

Two weeks later on board an inter-island boat heading south for the island of Mindanao to our business conference, Anne and I were into anything exotic. We stood at the rail in the moonlight eating mangos, then we went below and extravagantly ordered a Coke. Laurie Reid, one of the men who had just finished the language survey, introduced himself and started telling us about the Balangaos, the people who lived a two-days' hike beyond the end of the road.

The more he talked, the more we could imagine hiking up mountains through rain forests and breaking through into neatly terraced valleys where people lived in houses on stilts. The children in his photographs gazed out at us from huge, dark eyes; their hair was thick and shiny and black.

By tradition, Balangaos were headhunters, although, for the most part, that tradition was stifled. The men still wore G-strings and the women wrap-around skirts woven on backstrap looms.

And these people wanted someone to live with them and write down their language. When the language survey showed that the seven thousand Balangaos needed their own translation of the Scriptures, some of the elders were asked if they would consider inviting Americans to live with them. Together they discussed the proposal and came to a group consensus.

Some thought maybe it would be good to have more white people in the valley. European priests had been in the area for ten years and they'd built the only high school in the Balangao world. Maybe these other white people would help them, too.

Besides, they'd liked the American GIs they'd met during World War II. The Americans had shared their rations with Balangaos and even had polished their own boots. They didn't force the Balangaos into hard, trail-blazing labor like some of the enemy foreigners their parents and grandparents told them about.

True, some of those enemy intruders had lost their heads—the Balangaos were good at revenge—but it still rankled their grandchildren that foreigners had come in and treated them that way.

But Americans were different; they had treated Balangaos with respect. Finally one of the elders spoke for the group. "Yes," he finally announced, "we'd like Americans to come and live with us."

As we heard more about the Balangaos and prayed for them, the two-day hike mattered less. The Spirit of God had captured our imaginations; need and adventure created a new dream for us.

Since Balangao was all we could think about, we announced to our director that we wanted to go there.

"Oh no," he said, "we're not sending women there. That place is too inaccessible."

"But not for us," we pleaded. "We can hike that far." We desperately wanted to go.

We talked and prayed about it some more. A few days later the director let us defend our sense of God's leading. We assured him we could manage. After making sure we really understood how hard it would be to travel there and to live there, he agreed to assign us to Balangao.

We happily bought supplies: bags of sugar, salt, and flour, cans of powdered milk and margarine, and a case of canned mackerel. We bought basins and soap, and got the blankets, towels, and sleeping bags we had brought in our barrels. Laurie, who had agreed to be our guide and introduce us to the Balangao people, helped us pile everything on an old bus and we headed out of Manila.

It took us three days to reach the end of the winding road. It seemed like the end of the world. The bus looked like an old country church with rows of wall-to-wall wooden benches for seats. One missing side was the permanently open door. It was nice and breezy—until it rained; then it was wet and muddy. In dry season, no matter what color people were when they got on the bus, when they got off, they were all the same dusty, light gray.

Each day found us a hundred years deeper into the past. The third evening we lurched to a stop in Barlig, a little town at the end of the road. Gracious people took our baggage off the roof of the bus and followed us into the rustic mountain inn. They stacked all our belongings in our room and we fell onto the wooden-slat beds to make a stab at sleeping.

For the next two days, Laurie introduced us to the towns-people, including the local mayor, some teachers, and the priest. The mountain people of the Philippines are famous for their hospitality. The innkeepers cooked meals especially for us. It was always the same thing: rice cooked just the way they imagined Americans would like it—soft and moist—and a can of very expensive and very fancy Vienna sausages. They wouldn't serve us greens or black beans, like they ate, or even canned mackerel, a treat for most of them. No, they served us the best the town had to offer. We'd eat it somehow and drool as they ate the food they considered too humble for us: nice, firm rice and fragrant vegetables in broth.

Most of the men in the mountains understood the trade language, but only well enough to conduct simple business with outsiders. They didn't understand it well enough to grasp the deeper concepts such as those in Scripture. And the women understood even less—that's why we were going to Balangao.

Short, stocky men and women with rippling muscles agreed to carry our boxes and baggage along the two-day trail into Balangao. We started hiking. And climbing. And sometimes almost crawling. Straight up. Then down. First the trail switched back and forth, then it ran almost straight up the face of a mountain through rain forests.

We learned about leeches that first day. You rarely feel leeches fasten on you because they inject an anesthetic along with the anticoagulant that makes your blood flow freely. When they're full of blood they just drop off, but blood keeps oozing from the spot for hours. When we stopped to rest, Anne found her slip soaked with her own blood.

Clutching at roots to keep from falling off the mountain, we tipped our heads back to take in the tropical garden paradise of dainty orchids dripping from massive trees; the hike was a paradox of agony and beauty. We hiked in the rain over clay-mud trails as slick as ice. Exhausted, we finally came to the first village where we huddled for the night in a schoolteacher's smoke-filled mountain home.

Still exhausted the next morning, Anne and I never admitted how we felt, or that we might not be able to go on. That second day went on forever. We both dissolved into tears at times, but fortunately never at the same time. It helped to stop and eat our trail lunch: cold rice wrapped in banana leaves, a hard-boiled egg, and a damp bit of coarse salt in its own wrapper.

It took that whole next day to hike the rim of the Balangao valley, a giant bowl terraced from top to bottom with a staircase of fluorescent spring-green fields and gray rock walls. We were overlooking the eighth wonder of the world: the rice terraces. The houses were up on four-foot stilts; the walls were made of hand-hewn lumber and the roofs were thatched. The surrounding fields were dotted with miniature houses: the rice granaries. The valley was as magnificent as the rain forest.

Suddenly the trail turned into a rock-paved path that led us into the tidy mountain town of Natunin. We met the mayor, who invited us in, fed us more soft rice *and* what he, a prominent man, had stored for visitors of distinction: Vienna sausages. He gave us a whole room of his house to ourselves that night. We reveled in the luxury.

When we woke up the next day we couldn't believe we were actually *in* Balangao territory where we were going to translate the Scriptures—once we found a place to live. That day we hiked through that beautiful valley, through village after village of thirty or so tiny houses clumped together.

The trails were six-inch-wide dikes on the rims of rice terraces filled with mud and water; they sat on top of tall rock walls that sculptured the mountainsides. They were slippery even when dry. Often innocent-looking little clods of clay were ball bearings that could send feet flying up and sometimes off the narrow path. If we slipped off the trail on the uphill side, we'd be knee-deep in the mud. But if we fell off into the terraces we'd fall the height of the wall we were perched on—from five to twenty feet.

Late that afternoon we walked wearily into the very last village on our list, Botac. Our sneakers squished with mud from dips into the terraces. So far, a number of people had offered to move over and let us share part of their houses; but here they offered us the use of a whole house, huge by Balangao standards. It was one room fourteen feet wide and sixteen feet long and it even had a separate cooking house.

It was less than five minutes away from a bubbling spring of sparkling clean water.

This was ideal. Laurie talked to old Canao, the man in charge of the house and the one he'd dealt with before. We were presented to him as "those Americans you said you'd like to have come live with you."

Canao and the others were horrified. None of them had dreamed that the Americans coming to live with them would be women. In fact, none of them had ever seen white women. But…they had agreed to take Americans, and here we were. What could they do? They took us in.

5
I'll Be Your Father

That night Canao fed us dinner at his house. Laurie told us that when a Balangao, or a man from any other group in the surrounding mountains, fed a person in his home, it was his pledge to protect that person with his own life. Canao, the spokesman of the village, was taking a stand.

He came daily to supervise as we set up housekeeping. After we'd been there a few days he walked in looking quite serious, without a trace of his usual smile. He was outwardly calm, but we could feel his tension and heard it in his voice.

"Don't you realize it's not safe for women to be here? Don't you know we're headhunters?" He let that sink in and then, with a sigh, said, "You need someone to take care of you—I'll be your father!" He gave a short, deliberate nod, sealing his words with final authority.

We looked across the room at that wiry little man, barefoot and wearing tattered short pants. At five-foot-two, he probably didn't weigh much over one hundred pounds. Some missing front teeth made him lisp; we couldn't understand him very well. The few teeth he had were stained red from chewing betel nut. We knew he'd never even been to high school. He seemed a little pushy. He was always telling us what to do. He had already made up a list of words that he thought we needed to learn and had tested us on them.

Anne's beloved father, a doctor, had died when she was in high school. My strong dad was very alive on our California farm. *People don't have substitute fathers*, we thought.

So, forcing smiles, we compromised and reluctantly called him "uncle," hoping he wouldn't give us too much trouble. But Mariano Canao Lucasi was a perceptive man. He knew what we were thinking. And he was a wise man— he ignored it.

As we started to unpack, an ocean of Balangaos flooded our house. People came in any time they wanted, violating our American sense of privacy. They nonchalantly lifted box lids to see what was inside, oblivious to our value of private ownership, and gasped, "Imagine, an entire case of soap!"

Uncle Canao said, "Yes, and that's not all. You should see what they've stored up in the ceiling!" The few small boxes of canned goods we'd brought in to last us the next three months were an unimaginable fortune to them.

Our initiation into the Balangao language and culture began as day and night people crowded around us teaching us words and correcting our pronunciation. Every night after supper Uncle Canao came to teach us.

Five days after our arrival, I was called to deliver a baby. I climbed up the bamboo ladder and found the baby girl already born. She was stillborn—the first dead baby I'd ever seen. Emotion drained out of me as I reached down, picked the baby up, cut the cord, and wrapped her in a blanket. I laid her on the floor next to her mother and I ached for everyone. The mother just lay there, lifeless.

Where are the midwives? I wondered. *Why is no one helping her?* All the women just sat nearby, looking helpless and frantic. I'd scrubbed for a few deliveries in a medical missionary course, but I didn't know much. My experience delivering babies was limited. I massaged her uterus, found the "ball" under my hand, and gently pushed the placenta out. Relieved and astonished, the watching women couldn't believe how easily the placenta came out. They'd never seen such a thing. Instantly I'd found a special place in these lives and hearts. That act marked the beginning of my career of delivering their babies and saving their mothers.

Over and over again, the Balangaos asked, "Why have you come?" And over and over again we answered, "We've come to translate God's Word into your language, and teach you to read it, so you can know God."

"Yes, but why have you come?"

Everyone asked us the same question, some repeatedly—and we always answered the same way. But it never made any sense to them. Years later we found out they'd finally decided we must have come for one of two reasons: either to get their language and sell it in America, which would explain why we kept writing it down; or to look for husbands, since we didn't have any.

Under Uncle Canao's watchful direction, everyone helped take care of us and our strange needs: they built us an outhouse (though they couldn't imagine why we wanted to save that stuff); they put up the antennae for our radio; and, with months of hard labor interspersed with bouts of intense deliberations, they built our airstrip.

Uncle Canao helped us every step of the way, though at first we occasionally questioned his advice. He told us not to pay people for helping us learn the language. When we wanted to give people used clothing—and they needed it—he warned us not to do it. "If you give things away, people will hate you because you'll never be able to distribute them equally." So we reluctantly sold our used clothing for a pittance.

When we insisted on paying wages to get our airstrip built or our wooden floors polished, he set the price for us. If we paid too much, he explained we'd ruin the pay scale and everyone would be angry. Many translators didn't have anyone giving them such good advice. They learned these things the hard way. Soon Uncle Canao proved himself to us, and whatever he suggested, we did.

So when he asked us to go to a peace pact celebration with him, we went. Barefoot men and women were dressed in their Balangao finest: intricately patterned bright blue and red G-strings and skirts. The women wore their inherited wealth: necklaces of ancient Chinese beads made of pottery and stone. The men were bare-chested and those who had taken heads had chest tattoos.

The men sang and chanted and burst into impromptu, warbling song-chants to negotiate the peace pact. At one point Uncle Canao broke into song; he chanted that we were his daughters and we ate in his house. He was announcing that all the rules that guarded Balangaos were guarding us.

Once the agreements were made, everyone joined in the celebration. Gripping handles made of human jaw bones, three men at a time played polished brass gongs. They beat them in an enticing rhythm that rang out across the valley. Anne and I were called to join the circle of dancers; she jumped right in, following the older women's subtle steps, head down, white arms extended like their tattooed ones. I was right after her.

Inside their houses we sat on the floor and outside we tried to squat with them, drinking coffee, eating boiled pig and sticky-rice cakes, and listening to people recount the solemn agreements that had forged the latest peace pact between two warring mountain peoples.

These peace pacts put an end to fighting and revenge killing between the two groups. Members of each group could hike through the other's territories, intermarry, and work together without fearing ambush and attack—until someone broke the pact.

Without a peace pact there was no safety for either group outside of their own territory. In fact, before Anne and I hiked back out to the road the first time, Uncle Canao warned us not to tell anyone on the trail that we were from Balangao. The person asking us might be a member of a warring group who would take revenge on Balangao through us.

Within a few months our ability to speak Balangao crept ahead of their ability to speak English, so we switched to speaking Balangao. In Balangao it was only proper for us to call Canao "Ama"—Father. And saying it in Balangao sounded right. Uncle Canao became Ama.

In those days we had just a glimmer of understanding about God's gift to us through Ama. We didn't comprehend that our new family was Mark 10:29 coming true for us. God was giving back to us what we'd left for his sake.

6
Sacrifices and Spirits

Ama said it was too bad we were women—if only we were men we'd learn the language faster. "But," he advised, "if you just eat more rice you'll learn our language better." He was right about the rice—the more we ate, the better we spoke Balangao.

We'd hike over the terraces to different villages, walk past their dogs—barking skeletons with curled-up tails—and climb up little bamboo ladders into dark, smoke-filled houses. Looking down through the cracks in the floor we could see black, bristly-haired pigs rooting around and chickens scratching for any tidbit of rice that might have dropped through the floor.

Sitting on their polished wooden floors by open fires, we ate the world's best rice with our fingers and drank strong, black, home-grown coffee—and we learned to speak Balangao. We also learned what troubled Balangaos: they talked about their problems and their fears, and they always talked about the evil spirits. The evil spirits ruled the Balangaos' lives by their unceasing demands for sacrifice.

If a man went to the forest to get firewood and he accidentally stepped on one of the spirit's houses, or worse, on one of the spirit's children, he'd have to sacrifice a chicken or pig. The Balangaos knew when they'd offended a spirit because when they got home they'd find a child sick or something else wrong. They had to sacrifice to make amends.

The appearance of a rainbow, an omen of imminent evil, struck terror in everyone. It meant they'd have to sacrifice. If one appeared while they were building a house, even if they were tying on the very last shelf inside, they'd have to tear the house down, right to the ground.

Mothers often put taro leaves in their children's hair when they left the house. They believed it would trick the spirits into thinking the children were the toxic taro plant and so leave them alone.

Bird omens also controlled their lives. Three days in a row we watched one of our neighbors head for the forest to hunt, only to return home—the calls of certain birds had warned him of impending danger. No one dared defy the omen birds.

Dreams were even worse. If they dreamed about a child who was sleeping in the room with them, that child would surely die unless they sacrificed a water buffalo in exchange for his life.

Balangaos couldn't proceed with marriage plans when a butchered animal's bile forbade it. They didn't dare say their mother-in-law's name or they'd get a boil. When a child fell, someone would throw water on the spot and call to his soul to return. Inggay, our neighbor, announced her newborn son was a daughter in order to fool the evil spirits who had let her daughters live. The spirits had taken all but one of her sons.

Balangaos struggled to produce enough food for themselves and to raise enough pigs and chickens to keep the spirits pacified so they would let their children live. Sometimes an entire extended family's resources were tapped to satisfy the spirits' demands.

If the sacrifice required a water buffalo, they'd go from relative to relative collecting enough money and valuables to purchase such an expensive animal. No blood relative, no matter how distantly related, ever would refuse to give what he or she had to help another relative meet the spirits' demands.

When we arrived, the only meat Balangaos had ever eaten was that left by the spirits after a sacrifice. They'd call to us, "Come and eat what the spirits left." It took blood to call the spirits. When these spirits came, they'd demand additional sacrifices. But the spirits would just take the animal's spirit and leave the flesh for the people. Balangaos explained to us, "Spirit eats spirit and flesh eats flesh."

Even when their demands were met, the spirits often took the Balangaos' children or crops. The spirits would speak through a medium to explain that the sacrifice had been inadequate. They never gave any reasons and the Balangaos never expected any. Ama and his wife, Ina, had lost six of their twelve children—in spite of trying to meet every demand the spirits made. For years Ina lived in a fog of grief as one child after another died. The spirits only looked out for their own needs; they never cared about the Balangaos' grief or poverty. They had more power than people did and were never to be questioned.

When someone was sick, relatives and neighbors would crowd around with endless questions. No one asked about the secondary cause of the illness, "Is this typhoid fever?" or "Is this tuberculosis?" Instead, they searched for the primary reason: "How did he offend the spirits?" And they'd try to guess what happened.

"Maybe he stepped on a spirit in the forest."

"Ah, maybe she went by a tree where the spirit lived."

"Oh, maybe the lightning ate her."

Everyone was allowed to speculate. Then they'd call a medium to their home to learn how the spirits had been offended. Only a spirit speaking through a medium could name the offense and the sacrifice to atone for it.

The medium would crouch under or inside the house of the one who was sick, huddle over a chicken, kill it, and use its blood to call the spirits.

I'll never forget the first time Anne and I saw the spirits possess someone. We hadn't been living in Botac long when little Aglipay contracted pneumonia. I'd given him an injection of penicillin, but the spirits, speaking through a medium, told the parents to not allow their son to have another injection. The third day his breathing was labored; it became precariously shallow and slow. He was gasping for air just three or four times a minute. Obviously, he couldn't last much longer.

The old spirit medium was called and sacrifices were made. She called the spirits, by name, to come; she convulsed and shook; then, stiff as a board, she passed out. They caught her as she fell over. People gathered around her and when she came to, they started asking the spirits questions.

"What have we done wrong?"

"What do you want for payment?"

"What do you want for sacrifice?"

Then the woman spoke in a male spirit's voice. The spirits simply wanted some pigs and chickens, so they had made the boy sick to get his parents' attention. In exchange for the boy's life, they'd accept three pigs, two chickens, and some rice and wine and beads. The father was immensely relieved; he could meet the spirits' demands.

The negotiations were finished and with violent wrenching the spirits left the medium. Dazed, she grabbed her sore throat with one hand and her aching head with the other.

The men scurried to kill the animals and offer their souls to the spirits.

The dying child was well by the next day.

I was dumbfounded. *These spirits really do have power*, I thought. It was the spookiest thing I'd ever seen. Small wonder people argued against following God's way: "If we stop sacrificing, what will we do when our children are sick? Just let them die?"

But there was one person in Botac who did not sacrifice to the spirits. Only one. Tekla, the only living child of the most powerful spirit medium in all of Balangao, refused to sacrifice.

7
I Wish I Could Know God

The Balangaos believed that Tekla's father, Uyyama, was a descendant of a spirit. Long ago one of his ancestors had married a beautiful girl he found in a cave in the forest—the "daughter of a spirit" living in the mountains. The remains of that mountain spirit lived in a bamboo tube called the *toeto*. And, for a price, the spirit wielded power on behalf of its caretaker.

Despite Uyyama's powerful heritage, six of his seven children had died. In a desperate attempt to save Tekla, his last child, he sold his soul and agreed to be the caretaker of the *toeto*. The bamboo tube sat inside a clay pot that hung prominently from the rafters of his house. It spoke on its own. Uyyama gave the spirit gifts of chickens and eggs.

53

Tekla did survive her childhood and Uyyama felt his service to the *toeto* was worthwhile, but Tekla herself would not sacrifice to the spirits. When she was a little girl an itinerant priest had visited the area. He showed everyone a picture of an angel watching over some small children. This priest told them about a great God in heaven who had angels that protected children. From that day Tekla longed to know the God who loved little children. But her friends taunted her, saying, "You can't be a Christian. You're a descendant of an evil spirit."

The itinerant priest came by from time to time and after he'd leave, groups of people would gather in houses to discuss what they'd heard. Listening on the fringes, Tekla learned the Christian prayers, and later she even taught them to others. But she never felt she really knew God. Something was missing. "Maybe if I don't sacrifice," she thought, "maybe then God will come to me."

Tekla grew up, married a man named Tony, and had children. The spirits pursued her relentlessly, but she refused to sacrifice—even when her children were sick. This infuriated her father. Didn't she love her children? Didn't she care if they died? The spirits brought her endless sicknesses and tried to kill her. When deathly ill, she'd have people carry her from house to house to evade the spirits, but they always managed to follow her. Not everyone saw them, but Tekla did. They appeared as huge, black monstrous dogs or wild beasts. She threw dirt in their eyes, but they still kept appearing to her and talking to her.

Tekla was seriously considering sacrificing. She was almost ready to give up. "Maybe I can never really know God," she thought. "Maybe I need to sacrifice and come to terms with the spirits."

And then Anne and I came.

We had wondered if *anybody* would ever understand why we'd come. So when Tekla asked, Anne and I just sighed and mumbled, "We've come to put God's words in a Book, and teach you to read, so you can know God."

"Know God!" she gasped. "Oh, I wish I could know God!" We couldn't believe our ears—did someone finally understand?

Tekla spent countless hours with us those first months. Anne and I would struggle to teach her about God and she would help us learn Balangao. We would squat next to her in front of the firebox in her house while she cooked. "*Nokaychi?* (What's that)?" we asked, pointing to the fire. "*Apoy,*" she answered. As she blew on the fire through a bamboo tube, I pulled out a notebook and pen from the big pocket on my skirt and wrote the word down.

"*Nokaychi?*" we asked, pointing to the small bundles of golden rice drying above the fire. "*Pagey,*" she answered. Two of her children took some of those bundles outside and put them in a huge mortar. Then they reached up under the house for two five-foot-long ironwood pestles and with one child on each side, they pounded the rice. By late afternoon the whole village resounded with the thudding of women and children pounding rice for dinner.

Later her children put the pounded rice in a large, flat basket, shook it, and tossed it rhythmically. The creamy, fat kernels of rice stayed in the middle of the basket and the bran danced over to the edge and hopped out of the basket. *"Nokaychi?"* I asked, pointing to a chicken pecking in the pile of bran. *"Mano,"* she answered.

As Anne and I learned the language, Tekla learned about God's love and power. Over and over we discussed the parables and the Gospels. She even helped us translate the Christmas story into a play. But information about God wasn't enough. Every day ended with Tekla's same sigh: "I wish I could know God."

Frustrated, I wondered, *Which words will work that miracle in Tekla's heart and help her understand about God?*

After a few months, Anne and I hiked out of the Balangao valley for a break and to replenish our supplies. We prayed for Tekla every day, knowing that only God could sort things out for her.

One day after we hiked the trails back to Botac, Anne was outside catching up on the news with Tekla while I cooked lunch over our kerosene burner. Breathless, Anne came flying to the house and, leaping up on the porch, she said, "Guess what Tekla's saying now? She's saying, 'How different my life is, since God has come to me.'"

Suddenly, Tekla radiated joy. "I can actually talk to God in Balangao, my own language," she said. "I can even tell him my fears. He's my protector; he's more powerful than the spirits. And he isn't like them: he doesn't lie and he doesn't need my pigs and chickens like they do. I actually matter to him!"

Tekla had heard God's voice. God himself had gotten through to her. Tekla had heard his offer of salvation and realized that even she, the descendant of an evil spirit, could ask God into her life. And God, indeed, came into her. She was ecstatic. And we were amazed.

Tekla, with others, helped us formulate an alphabet consisting of seven vowels and fifteen consonants. She also introduced us to rice planting and harvesting. We gingerly followed her into the rice fields, cringing in the knee-deep mud. Later she showed us how salt would make field leeches drop off our legs.

Tekla also took us to her garden on the side of the mountain where we picked and peeled fresh pineapple. We sat down, facing the majestic rice terraces. As we ate pineapple, the juice ran down our arms and dripped off our elbows. No king ever ate any fruit as sweet as the pineapple that grows on the mountainsides of Balangao.

Tekla paid a high price for her friendship with us. Balangaos maintain close relationships within their group. In their view one of the worst things that can happen is to be set apart from the rest of their group. Jealous of Tekla's growing friendship with us, the other Balangaos punished her with cutting words to draw her into line. "Fortunate you," they slyly remarked to her. That one phrase was both a malicious accusation and a proclamation of exclusion. They tried to press her about the gifts they thought we gave her and the money she must be acquiring because of us.

Before we came, the Balangaos had treated Tekla as different because she wouldn't sacrifice. Now Tekla's differences were even more obvious and her position as a viable member of Balangao society was being threatened.

Finally, one evening when I was by myself in Balangao, Tekla came to me almost in tears. She couldn't take any more. Fumbling with words, she said, "Let's try not to be so close for a while…Maybe if you didn't come to my house so often…I just can't stand the talk."

I told Tekla I understood and that I'd just eat in my own house, but I was devastated. I'd come to Balangao to help people, but now our relationship was hurting Tekla, even destroying her. I'd come, longing to bring life and hope, but instead I was bringing fire down on her head. It made me realize Ama must be bearing the brunt of that kind of gossip, too, since I was often at his house. What was I doing to these people?

It didn't occur to me that the Gospel could cause pain. I concluded I must be doing something wrong. If I were doing it right, *why* were people getting hurt?

Choosing reason over emotion, I resolved to tell Ina and Ama that I didn't need a family anymore. *Enough of this family situation*, I said to myself, trying to be strong and brave. *I'll just dissolve it and live neutrally with everyone.*

I suspected that Ama, like Tekla, would welcome a way out of this dilemma, a release from this burden. But I had to free him in such a way that he wouldn't be ashamed. I would approach the idea as if it were just the next phase in the process.

I planned out everything I would say: "You've been a great family; you've gotten me over the rough parts and you've taught me to speak Balangao. Now it's time for me to branch out and carry on by myself. Let's just cut the family ties. I don't really need a family now. I think it would be better if I belonged to everybody...."

The next day Ama came over for a glass of cold water. Leaning there on the wall, he had grown to be six feet tall in my eyes and his lisp had vanished from my ears—he was strength and wisdom. I'd have to do this well. I took a deep breath. Cool and nonchalant, I began my speech. I actually thought I was doing a rather fair job of it when he cut me short.

He stood straight up, set the glass on my desk, and looked me straight in the eye, saying, "You are talking foolishness. What you are saying is impossible. You are my daughter, and you will always be my daughter!" My mouth fell open. Caught off guard, I got teary.

He went on, "You just cannot listen to the talk of the people. I don't adjust myself according to what people say. Gossip doesn't draw blood. It's the nature of people to gossip." He went on with more, and ended with, "And that is settled!" And it was.

Later I heard that when people accused him of receiving gifts of used clothing from me, he'd say, "Right, I have trunks full of clothes. Just come on over and see."

Tekla never pulled away, either. I'm not sure why. Maybe she just followed Ama's example.

In Balangao I learned the true meaning of the word *family*. "Family" is where you belong, no matter what. I grew up in Balangao.

8

You Might Get Lonely

Over and over I explained to the Balangaos that Jesus Christ is stronger than the spirits. They listened politely, but experience had taught them it was foolhardy not to give the spirits what they wanted: sacrifice or suffer the consequences. I'd seen what the spirits could do. Even I knew the reality of their power.

Every day I told Ama about Jesus Christ. He'd nod or mumble in reply, "We're Christians—we've been baptized." He tried hard to keep everybody happy; he'd been baptized by the priests in order to please God, and God wasn't giving him any trouble. But now he had to work hard to keep the spirits satisfied; they always created trouble. My frustration grew.

Anne and I had been there for a year when we were scheduled to attend a linguistic workshop in faraway Nasuli on the southern island of Mindanao. We needed a language assistant, but all the Balangao people were busy in the fields. The women were preparing the fields for planting and the men were repairing the rock walls that supported the rice terraces.

Some estimate that if those terrace walls were placed end to end, they would stretch around the world. Each rock is carefully chosen to interlock with all the rocks surrounding it. When repairing a badly damaged wall, the Balangaos carry rocks from the riverbed, lay them on the ground near the wall, and puzzle over where to put each rock. Since they don't use mortar, the rocks must fit exactly so they sometimes chip away at a rock to make it fit. They take great pride in building a wall that stands strong, even against typhoons.

Since none of the others would leave their fields for so long, Ama felt obliged to go with us: we were his daughters, his responsibility. His work would have to wait.

Ama had never been on the open sea until we got on the inter-island boat to Mindanao. All day long he stood at the back of that boat as it made its way through the South China Sea and he never saw any land. Finally he shook his head at the blue expanse and said, "They told us in school that the water was more than the land, but I never believed them until now."

At the workshop Ama made friends with language assistants from all over the Philippines. They communicated with each other by sheer determination, even when they could not understand any of the other person's language. Ama met many different groups of people, including one group he had always thought were mythical.

Those friendships were his travel ticket through all parts of the Philippines. It wasn't safe for Balangaos to travel alone through some areas, but if they had a friend from that area accompanying them and housing them for the night, they were safe. Ama told me, "I bet now I could go just about anywhere in the whole world, and I'd have a place to stay."

A man of integrity and responsibility, Ama also possessed a sense of humor. Once when Anne and I were in a lowland town where a more prestigious trade language was spoken, we stood speaking Balangao with him. Bystanders were wide-eyed as they watched these tall, white women talking to this little Balangao man—in his language.

Finally one sidled up to him and asked how it was that we could speak his language. Eyes twinkling, he said, "Of course they can speak my language; they're my daughters. Their mother is in America."

As I got to know him better, my love grew for this man. I desperately wanted Ama to believe in Jesus Christ. *If only I could figure out how to say it right, maybe then he'd believe.*

In fact Ama was as perplexed as anyone else over why we had really come to Balangao; somehow we weren't communicating to him. But God knew how to reach this man. God knew that Balangaos understand dreams...and Ama had a dream. In it he was walking to the river when he saw a Balangao man he didn't know. This gave the dream an air of mystery because Ama knew everyone in Balangao. Ama walked up to the stranger and asked him, "Just why have those American children come here, anyway?"

The stranger answered, "They have come to tell you something that is more enduring than a great, mighty rock. You must believe what they tell you." Then Ama woke up.

For years, he didn't tell us about his dream, but it was that dream that confirmed the message that our faltering words and cultural mistakes were obscuring. His thinking turned in a new direction.

I'd been away for another linguistic workshop and was back in Botac starting to unpack my suitcases when Anne quietly said, "I have something to tell you."

It was late afternoon and people were everywhere. Home from the fields, they were splitting firewood, pounding and winnowing rice, and preparing dinner. The woven walls and open windows of houses sitting right next to one another didn't afford any privacy, so Anne and I went upstream to an isolated area far from any trails where we could take our evening bath and talk.

The Balangaos bathed at the spring in the very early morning or under cover of night. But we always felt our white skin was too conspicuous—especially after one man told us that a white man in a G-string would look like a tree without any bark. We *always* found private places to bathe.

Anne sat submerged in the river with a bar of soap in her hand, and told me that while I was gone she'd been getting letters from Tommy Hopkins. Recently Tommy had found out what commitment to God was all about. He'd written to Anne, "Now I am free to ask you to marry me."

In one of those rare experiences, I was flooded with assurance that this was God's plan. I loved Anne, and I knew how much she loved Tommy and that he loved her. A hopeless romantic, I couldn't imagine a better gift for her than Tommy, even though I'd never met him.

Ironically, Anne wasn't so sure. She didn't know what to do. She asked, "How can I leave these Balangao people I love? How can I leave you all alone? What about my linguistics training and the people who sent me to be a translator?"

All good reasons to stay, I thought, *except for the best reason to go: it's God's will.* We sat talking in the river for a long time. Anne cried.

Suddenly, a man rounded the bend right in the middle of the stream, nearly on top of us. We froze, speechless. We were two trees with absolutely no bark! We didn't know what to do...but he did. Eyes forward, he tipped his hat, walked right between us, and continued on his way, indifferently. We were doing the right thing in the right place, and from his point of view there was nothing to be embarrassed about.

We laughed until we cried trying to imagine what our mothers would say if they knew. Still laughing, we returned to our house where Anne spent days thinking and praying about what she should do.

Weeks later, Anne flew to the United States with some lingering doubts about leaving Balangao. But when she stepped off the plane and saw Tommy, God gave her the assurance he'd given me in the beginning. Every doubt vanished. Two months later they were married.

I tried hard not to make any ripples, hoping the administrators wouldn't change my program since I didn't have a partner. Our policy didn't allow a woman to live in a remote place alone. But they let me stay in Balangao because of three things: my close relationship with Ama and Ina; the completed airstrip, which traded the two-day hike for a twenty-one-minute flight; and the agreement that I would fly out of the village for a break at least once every four weeks.

Right after Anne left, Ama marched over to my house and said, "From now on, you'll eat all your meals at our house. If you stay by yourself, you'll get lonely; if you get lonely, you'll go home just like Anni did; and if you go home, who will give us medicine?" I could have resisted their food, but that kind of love was irresistible.

Then Ama told me to get a piece of paper; he had a letter to dictate—to my parents. He told them he realized how they must feel with their daughter so far away. He assured them of my safety and he pledged himself to care for me. And Ama was a man of his word.

I knew it would strain resources for Ama and Ina to provide three meals a day for me, their American daughter. *Should I buy special things they can't afford, and thereby imply their provision isn't adequate?* But I didn't want to be a guest; I wanted to be family. So we found the delicate balance—I furnished untold cans of mackerel.

We ate rice three meals a day and most often we had something to go with it. In cabbage season, we had cabbage; in bean season, we had beans; in greens season, we had greens; the rest of the time we had exotic fare.

One night I climbed up the ladder and saw that the only thing Ina had to go with our rice was a big, white enamel bowl full of shiny, roasted beetles. I quietly gulped. *How will I do on this one?* Awkwardly, I said to my four-year-old sister, Celia, "I don't know how to eat these. Will you show me?" Delighted, she picked out a big, fat one, plucked its legs off, pulled its sticker out, and popped the whole thing into her mouth.

I hoped no one would notice my trembling hand as I reached into the bowl and managed to pick up one of those creatures. I got the legs off and the sticker out, and, fighting inner resistance, I looked hard to the left and nonchalantly slipped it into my mouth from the right. I chewed. To my surprise, the beetle had a crunchy, fried taste; it actually tasted good!

More than once I tried hard to think about other things while I ate such delicacies. And my family always watched and wondered if they were caring well enough for their American daughter.

One evening during hot season before the first harvest was in, there were no vegetables available. My boxes were empty, and there wasn't even fern from the forest or snails from the rice paddies. That night dinner was rice and salt. I knew this was harder on them than it was on me, so I ate lots of rice. Even today my adopted brother, Doming, who was fifteen then, talks about how I ate just rice and salt with them and never complained. I truly belonged.

Ama wasn't the only one who was worried that I might get lonely. Unknown to me, the whole village had conspired to keep me company so I wouldn't get lonely and leave. All I knew was that people were always at my house—all day long. It was driving me crazy. I was working on my first translation project, selected portions from the Gospels, and I wanted to finish it. In desperation, I rudely left visitors standing alone while I went back to my desk to work. Eventually things returned to normal.

While I wasn't lonely with Anne gone, I did depend more on my Balangao family for help, advice, and companionship. One night a bunch of men came carrying Ama home and dumped him on the floor. He was drunk. That didn't happen often, but when it did I hated it. He felt that getting drunk was just something all men did, but it embarrassed me.

The next day I was furious. As I turned to where he lay, crumpled on the floor, I said, "Now what am I going to do? You're my father, and you're supposed to advise me. But when you're drunk, I don't have anyone to go to—what am

I going to do?" Then I turned and ran down the ladder and out of his house.

He never drank again.

9
My Child, It's Impossible

A few months later one of our planes got banged up landing on our airstrip. Before the pilot could finish repairing it, a typhoon picked it up like a dead dragonfly and slammed it on its back, badly damaging it.

After weeks of negotiations, our pilots got a helicopter to airlift the fuselage out, but it couldn't take the wings. Those planes are so small it's hard to believe that their wings are fully six feet wide and twenty feet long.

Months passed and my dilemma grew. If we could get the wings out, our aviation department could fix the airplane, which served all the translators in the northern Philippines. Pilot Wayne Aeschliman suggested: "Maybe you could arrange for the Balangaos to carry the wings out over the trail?"

It was only a suggestion. But for me, need plus a suggestion meant a command. The Balangaos called Wayne, "Mr. Wayne." That was their affectionate but respectful compromise between Wayne which seemed too familiar, and Mr. Aeschliman which seemed too formal. I told the Balangaos, "Mr. Wayne needs those wings. We've got to carry them out for him."

They agreed—they'd do almost anything for Mr. Wayne. They went to test the wings to see how they could carry them, but they came home sadly. "Juami," they said, "it can't be done."

I knew the trail was muddy, only one-man wide, fiercely steep and winding, and blocked by all kinds of trees and vegetation. But "can't" was never an option for me.

Ama spoke for the other Balangao men. "My child, it's impossible. We can't carry the wings out."

Still, I couldn't let go of the idea; there must be a way. My father's philosophy had become my own: "You can do anything you want to, you just have to work hard to do it." We had to help Wayne. We had to get those wings out.

I remembered all the times Wayne and his wife Marilyn had gone out of their way for me. Marilyn bought food and supplies for us and Wayne flew them in. Wayne would fly in to Balangao and stay overnight to fix my generator, plus anything else that happened to need repair at the time.

After Anne left, Marilyn was my special friend and confidante. When I was in Bagabag, we'd talk for hours. But I was always shy about including myself in their family at mealtime; I thought maybe I was intruding. But one day when I didn't come after Marilyn invited me to dinner, Wayne came striding over to my house and said, "We're not going to eat until you get over here!"

I just melted. They wanted me; I wasn't intruding.

Wayne helped the Balangao people, too. He flew salt, sugar, and kerosene into the village, and he flew sick people out. Then he and Marilyn drove the patients to the hospital and often kept them and their families in their own four-bedroom house.

Wayne reminded me of Anne: he, too, had absolute respect for each person, and never made a distinction because of social station. When Wayne promised a farmer he'd bring his salt on the plane the next day, he was there right when he said he would be. His word was good as gold. Quickly Wayne earned the name of Fanna—a Balangao mythical hero.

That wasn't too surprising, because Anne and I had been called The Magic People. They told us, "We knew you'd come some day. We've got stories about you. You're The Magic People. The Magic People can sit in their houses and have rice to eat without ever going to a rice field and soaking their legs in the mud. The Magic People have fires for cooking, though they never go to the forest for firewood."

The Balangaos watched us talk on the two-way radio. "The Magic People can talk to people in far-away villages without hiking the trail to get there."

And when the airstrip was finished, they said, "Ah, we have stories about you. The Magic People can fly through the air. So you're The Magic People. We knew you'd come someday."

But magic or not, I couldn't get those wings out of Balangao. I worried and thought about those airplane wings. I was caught between Wayne's need to get the plane fixed and what was possible for the Balangaos to do. I felt trapped between my Balangao friends and my co-workers. Letting Wayne down was not an option for me.

When I lost my appetite, the Balangaos were really afraid. Their diet is so minimal that they live on the edge of starvation. They literally do not have any reserves, and eating is critical to their health. If a person is sick, they'll always say, "Eat, eat!"

One evening at dinner Ama noticed I just picked at my food. Finally he said, "Oh, I wish you had a brother, then he could worry about these problems and take care of them for you."

That undid me. I lost control. "But, you're the only brothers I have," I said and then I started sobbing. "I'm OK...please don't worry. I'm going to be OK. I'll just go home now." And I ran home. But they were afraid. They ran across the fields and called Tekla to come comfort me.

Just the week before they'd called me to comfort her when she was inconsolable over a family problem. Balangaos believe that people can die from grief or despair. They couldn't understand why getting the airplane wings out meant so much to me, but they were afraid I might die.

My Child, It's Impossible

As I lay in my bed that night, I felt guilt about my outburst. It was unfair to put pressure on them and I was embarrassed that I hadn't controlled my emotions. I slept fitfully all night long and every time I woke up, I heard people talking next door, repeating my name.

The next morning I felt awkward when I went over to Ama's house for breakfast. I climbed the ladder, went over to the firebox and poured coffee out of a blackened pot into a tin cup.

Ama was reading a magazine I'd brought him, and never even looked up when he said matter-of-factly, "We're going to carry the wings out." The elders had concluded they had to do it or risk my life.

Another village helped. A pilot, Bill Foster, had flown a teenage boy and his father from that village to the hospital. Stranded in Bagabag by a typhoon, the father and son lived and ate with the Fosters. They tasted bread for the first time and polished off a whole loaf at each meal. Sharing food with someone is symbolic to Balangaos. They felt a strong debt of gratitude to "Mr. Bill."

In the Balangao culture, any kind of indebtedness is a powerful tie, binding lives together, weaving in interdependency and commitment. They always remember their debts. In fact, Balangaos will intentionally put themselves in debt to another person, just to forge a friendship.

The people in this village saw me as part of Bill's extended family. So when they heard about the wings, they said, "That Mr. Bill, he's our brother. We'll carry the other wing out."

Twenty volunteers were assigned to each wing. Working in six-man shifts, they carried each wing in a giant sling along those narrow trails that switchbacked straight up and down the mountains and across rivers. The men who weren't carrying cleared jungle brush from the trail and chopped down trees that prevented the wings from navigating the tight corners of the trail meant only for small, barefoot hikers. They carried the wings along eight miles of difficult trail and another twenty miles of easier terrain.

Three days later Wayne and I met the Balangaos at the end of the trail. They came limping over to the road with swollen feet and gouges in their shoulders where poles had cut into flesh. They crowded around us, nearly crippled; they'd done the impossible…for me.

Wayne was appalled when he saw them. Later he gently scolded me, "Why didn't you tell me it was impossible? We could have done something else. We could have even left the wings there."

Finally I understood. His suggestion wasn't meant to be a command. But it had been done. God took my mistake, and my weakness, and used it for his good. The Balangaos had done the impossible for me and I was indebted to them in a powerful way that bound us all together.

And Ama had won my heart forever.

10
Of Babies and Ambassadors

During my twenty years of living among the Balangao people, I was called to attend birth after birth in those dark, little houses. I soon learned that many of the women who'd died in childbirth had received no assistance at all. I taught the women how to breathe properly and how to assist the mother's delivery in order to prevent tearing. I also showed them how to massage the uterus, cut the cord, and clean up the baby. I dropped medicine in the baby's eyes and applied alcohol to the cord. Then I had fun: I dressed each baby in a brand new shirt and wrapped it in a soft, new blanket, gifts from my home church to the Balangao mothers.

Before I came, the Balangao women didn't have any idea of how to help during labor, but at least they offered their presence. They would crowd into the room and make sure the woman in labor didn't lie down or sleep. All the women who died in childbirth had slept at the end—maybe they wouldn't have died if they hadn't slept.

They'd hold the woman in a half-sitting position, fan her, and recount tales of tragedy after tragedy during delivery. They'd rub her legs and back, but they were careful not to give her anything to eat or drink the whole time she was in labor—even if it lasted for days. All they knew was what the spirits had taught their forefathers.

I used to tell them, "Oh, you poor people! Can't you see? The spirits just hate you and don't want you to live. They lie and tell you wrong things. They want you to die."

My words shocked them; they'd never questioned the spirits. They were afraid of them: spirits retaliate. And, sitting there on the floor, they'd look down and hug their knees more tightly. But they kept calling for my medical help. They said, "Our women don't die in childbirth since you've come."

Andrea was a childless woman who had lots of time to help us in the early days. She was free to teach us the language and help us translate.

But she desperately wanted children. I watched Balangaos perform almost every sacrifice they knew at Andrea's house as she and her husband bargained with the spirits for children. But nothing happened.

The Gospel of Mark was the first full book I attempted to translate. Andrea and I were working on chapter five of

Mark, where Jesus was casting out demons from a man, when Andrea interrupted me. "You translated that part wrong...people can't cast out demons. They come when they want, and they leave when they want. The demons are in control, not people."

Her eyes widened when I told her that Jesus wasn't an ordinary man. He was God and he was stronger than the spirits. She looked puzzled and confused, but continued helping me translate the Scriptures. Periodically she sacrificed to persuade the spirits to give her a baby.

Months later, Andrea casually mentioned that she now believed in this Jesus we'd been learning about in Mark. I made some noncommittal remark and thought, *You're just saying that because you know it's what I want to hear.* I thought it was her kind Balangao way of telling me she accepted me, strange beliefs and all. I simply didn't believe her.

Not many days later, Andrea, eyes glowing, made another announcement: "I'm going to have a baby."

"You're what?" I said. "H-h-how? What happened?"

She looked straight at me, "I *told* you I believe now. I decided to ask God for a baby and he's giving me one." I was floored. So she really did believe. We were both learning about God.

As Andrea's due date approached, so did the date for me to return to the United States to visit my family and the friends who were supporting me.

Andrea pleaded with me to delay my plans and deliver her baby before I left. I stroked her arm and reasoned with her, "But you know God now, dear sister. Just pray and ask the Lord for help and he will indeed help you."

With that, I flew out of Balangao to Bagabag, and within a few days I was due to be off to Manila and then California. It would be my first time home in five years. But Saturday an urgent request came over the radio to Bagabag. The United States ambassador wanted to visit a translation project.

Psychologically I was already halfway to California. *How can I go back to the village?* I thought. *I've got to pack to go to the States.* My mind raced. The worst part would be flying in to the village and out again in a matter of hours with no time to properly visit my Balangao friends.

I worked out a deal with our pilot: Bob Griffin never flew on Sundays, but he'd make an exception and fly me to Balangao on Sunday. He'd bring the ambassador on Monday morning and we'd all fly back to Bagabag Monday afternoon. *That's settled,* I thought, and I imagined the delight of my family when I suddenly reappeared after saying goodbye to them for a year.

My Balangao family members were in their fields when they heard the drone of the airplane. They dropped their hand hoes and ran for the airstrip. Everyone squealed, laughed, and joked about me coming back to stay. The visit was an unexpected gift to all of us.

That night Andrea went into labor. She had a long, hard labor before I was able to deliver her beautiful baby

Melisa. As I sat cross-legged on the floor rocking little Melisa and murmuring to her in Balangao, Andrea got a funny grin on her face. Nodding her head almost imperceptibly, she quietly told me, "I asked God to send you back to deliver my baby."

The next day, Monday, the ambassador changed his plans and canceled his trip. The plane came in to get me.

As I flew back to Bagabag in the little plane, I thought of what King Solomon said in Proverbs 21:1: "The king's heart (and the ambassador's) is in the hand of the Lord; he directs it like a watercourse wherever he pleases." God used an ambassador to answer the prayer of Andrea, his new child. That's just how he is.

11

Where Do We Go When We Die?

The people in my home churches in California kept throwing their arms around me and telling me they loved me and were proud of me. But I was distraught, thinking, *Even though I've got quaint stories to tell about cultural differences, that's not enough. These people have supported me for five years: they want "eternal fruit."* But only Tekla and Andrea had turned from the spirits to worship the living God. *Will they think it's been worth their investment?*

Then, not knowing what else to do, I unloaded my frustrations. "I just don't know what to do to make these people believe!" I said. "Even my own Balangao father doesn't believe in God." I told them about how the evil spirits had a

83

grip on the people's minds. They wanted to believe but were afraid of what would happen if they stopped appeasing the spirits.

The home team finally got the clear picture of the problem: we were in a spiritual battle, and our weapon was prayer. Simply praying, "God bless the missionaries," wasn't enough. They started praying as if life depended on their prayers. "God, show the Balangaos that you're stronger than the spirits. Make the Balangaos desire you; help them believe your Word."

After nine months in California I flew back to the Philippines. In Bagabag, I climbed into our small airplane and flew over barren hills and then jagged, green volcanic mountains to that tiny airstrip in the heart of Balangao. I could hardly wait to get to my Balangao home. I wanted to hold Andrea's miracle baby, Melisa. I was excited to see what God had done while I was gone. Maybe Melisa's birth, after Andrea's many years of infertility, would have proved to some of the Balangaos that God is loving and powerful.

My joy at getting back kept me from detecting the pall over the people who met me at the airstrip. Excitedly, we greeted, hugged, and after making arrangement for the cargo, raced down the trail to Botac.

But then I couldn't miss it. Crowds were gathered at Andrea's house. The news was finally whispered: little Melisa had been buried the day before I arrived.

No, No! my mind screamed. *Something is wrong. Surely God has made a mistake. Why, God? This baby can't die—she's an answer to our prayers! Why, God? Why?*

I blamed myself. Maybe if I'd come back sooner I could have saved Melisa. Somehow I was still assuming that if you obeyed God and he was helping you, things would always work out the way you wanted. I expected earth to be like heaven.

I was sure that any possibility of Balangaos ever believing in God had just been demolished. What would happen to Andrea's faith?

But it never occurred to Andrea to question God's right to do whatever he wanted. Balangaos understood the supernatural to be all powerful and never to be questioned. And that's how Andrea saw the God of heaven. Her grief had no anger mixed with it.

But the village gossip made Andrea afraid. Melisa hadn't been baptized and people told her she was probably in hell. I called Andrea away from the crowds. We sat together over coffee, secluded in my small kitchen, and I showed her from the Scriptures that baby Melisa was safe in heaven with Jesus and that we would see her again. Hope and peace helped ease the pain.

However, most people didn't understand, but Catholic tradition had taught them to meet every night for nine nights after the burial to pray prayers they had memorized in the trade language. I went to Andrea's house, too. Andrea had requested that I come because before they prayed they sat with the family talking late into the night, helping and comforting the bereaved. "Please come to my house and sit with me and tell the people where Melisa is now."

Their questions about death and Andrea's baby kept us all up long past bedtime. Balangaos traditionally knew very little about the next life, and what they did know was vague, but they wanted to know more because everyone spends so much time in the next world.

They asked, "Where do the dead go?"

"What's it like there?"

"Who is there?"

"Does everyone go there?"

Finally someone suggested we pray and all go home to bed.

I'd been waiting for that. Heart pounding, I asked, "Why do we pray? What are we going to pray for?" They were silent. They hadn't thought about that before. They had just memorized the prayers and they didn't really understand them.

Then someone asked, "Yes, why do we pray? What do the prayers mean, anyway?" After another hour of intense questions and answers, Andrea suggested we pray. I said, "Who is going to pray?" Everyone hemmed and hawed; they only knew memorized prayers. Finally they said, "You—you be the one to pray." It was my first public prayer.

In the Balangaos' own language, I thanked God for his mercy and his provision of heaven for baby Melisa. And I prayed for all the family, and that all the rest of us might know more and more of God.

Each night the people asked more questions. "Where do we go when we die? What about the resurrection?" I talked; I drew pictures on a little portable blackboard. On the ninth and last night we ate the traditional rice cakes; for us it was in celebration of Melisa being in heaven. Then they told me they wanted to continue studying; we could study the newly published Gospel of Mark. I had scarcely been back a week and Bible studies had started in Balangao!

How can one ever predict how God will bring himself glory? The heart-breaking, premature death of my friend's baby was God's avenue to answer my prayers, and the prayers of my friends back home in California.

I was still eating most of my meals at Ama's house, bombarding him with the Gospel—explaining, reasoning, and giving examples. He endured patiently, but didn't respond.

After a while the Bible studies following Melisa's death waned away. Then one day Ama casually picked up an English New Testament from my shipping-crate desk. He opened it to the first page, Matthew 1, which is a list of names. He stood frozen, staring at it. Incredulous, he asked me, "You mean this has a genealogy in it?"

I said, "Yeah, but just skip over that so you can get to the good part."

"You mean this is true?" he asked. Eyes riveted to the page, he struggled through the list of names.

Something's going on here! I got some shelf paper and made a genealogy from Adam to Jesus, from the ceiling clear down to the floor. Ama took it all over the village. He carefully explained, "We always thought it was the rock and the banana plant that gave birth to people. But we don't have their names written down. Look, here are ALL the names—written down!"

Balangaos had their own creation story, passed down from generation to generation through oral tradition. Ama told me their story:

> Long ago, when there were no people yet on the earth, the rock and the banana plant argued as to which of them would give birth to people and populate the earth. In the course of events, it was the frail banana plant from whom all the people of the earth descended. After producing fruit, the banana plant dies and new shoots spring up for succeeding generations. People have inherited all the frailty of the banana plant and are susceptible to all kinds of dangers and inevitably, death.

Although their story accounted for man's frailty, it didn't have their ancestors' names written down. A genealogy written was powerful. Balangaos loved that genealogy from the Gospel of Matthew. It proved the Bible was true: for the first time they had the actual names from the beginning of the world—written down.

Photo by Len Whalley

Canao and other Balangao elders agreed to have Americans come live with them—but were horrified when women showed up!

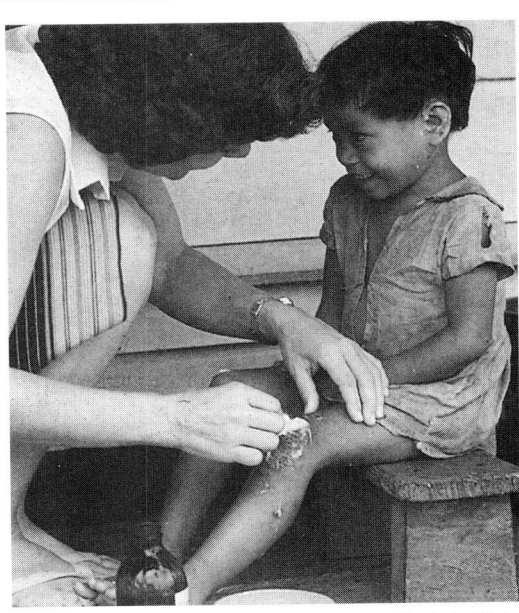

Right and bottom: Medical work opened doors and hearts. The Balangaos said, "Since you've come, our women don't die in childbirth."

Photo by Len Whalley

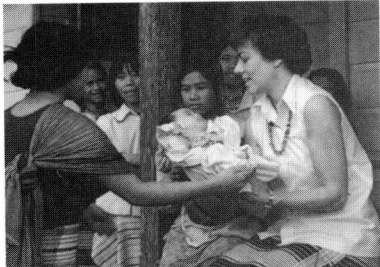

Photo by Hugh Steven

Photos by Hugh Steven

Sections of bamboo make good soup cups (and banana leaves good serving plates).

Right and middle: When someone got sick, **Chalinggay** would kill a chicken and use its blood to call the spirits.

Photos by Len Whalley

Right: The spirits demanded countless sacrifices of chickens and pigs. If they demanded a water buffalo, the entire extended family's resources were tapped to provide one.

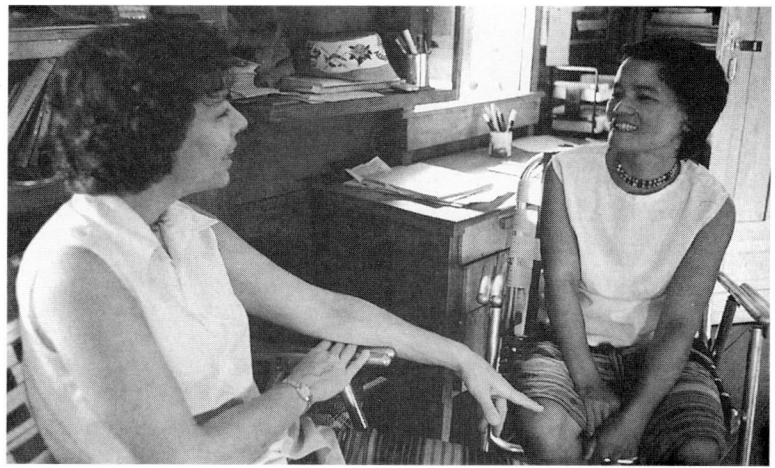

Photos by Len Whalley

Only **Tekla** refused to sacrifice to the spirits. From childhood, Tekla longed to know God. She spent countless hours teaching us her language while we struggled to teach her about God.

Photos by Len Whalley

Top: When **Canao** declared, "I'll be your father!" I never dreamed I'd soon call him father (**Ama**) and grow to love him like a father.

Right: Jesus's genealogy astounded **Ama**. He said, "We thought the rock and the banana plant gave birth to people. But look, here are all the names— written down."

Top: Little old **Forsan** was a spirit medium and very crippled, but she was also a fun eighty-year-old who loved to talk and gossip and joke! When she switched allegiance to serve God, the spirits tried to kill her.

Above: **Tekla's mother** was a dear soul! She was tiny, like most Balangaos, but her heart was enormous.

Left: True acceptance is having a child named after you. **Lolita** named her twin girls Joanne and Robyn. Wit' an arm around my namesake I'm coaching her mother, Lolita, on how to teach reading.

Photos by Len Whalley

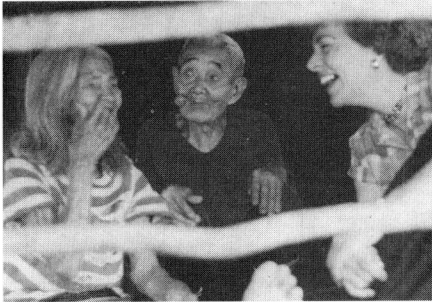

Photo by Debora Goodier

Top: My "little brother" **Doming,** interrupted his college education for a year to help finish the first draft of the New Testament.

Middle: After he believed, **Ama** went everywhere sharing the good news. His way of teaching was getting people to ask questions.

Left: The Balangaos are such friendly, warm, and fun-loving people!

Photos by John Walton

Top: When the Book finally came to Balangao, we had speeches, songs, gongs, dances, and lots of boiled pork for two days and nights! Hundreds of people sat on steps carved into the hillside, under a canopy of palm leaves, blankets, and tarps.

Middle and right: Each of those who helped in the translation received their prized copy. The very first one went to **Ama**.

12

A Church Is Born

◆━◇◇◆◇◇━◆

Since I'd taught Ama to read Balangao, I handed him a copy of 1 John, which I had translated and asked him to please correct the grammar. He started to read it and got excited. His excitement grew. Halfway through he said, "My child, these words are good! People would believe this if they could just hear it."

I stuttered, "Bu...bu...but that's my problem. What can we do so the people will hear these Words of God?" He didn't answer; fathers don't need to explain their plans to their daughters. He just excused himself and left, deep in thought.

The next Sunday, I was sitting at home when Ama walked in with a group of people. "Here we are," he said. "Teach us."

I wasn't sure what was going on. "Teach you what?"

"Teach us about that Word of God you translated," he said.

For the first time in six years, Ama was responding to the Word of God. For the rest of the morning they listened and interrupted with questions as I talked with them about God's Word. For the first time I had the official right to explain things to older people—that right was conferred on me by their questions. It opened their ears.

Their questions were clear:

"Where did people come from?"

"Where did sin come from?"

"Where did Satan come from?"

"If God is so powerful, and he likes us and he doesn't like Satan, why doesn't he get rid of him?"

"How does our sacrifice system compare with the sacrifices in the Bible?"

One man said, "Well, I'm a basket maker, and if I make a basket that turns out badly, I just burn it. Why didn't God do that with Satan?" They had difficult, philosophical questions. When they asked questions, they were forced to grapple with the truth. On and on the questions went.

They brought up their problems: dreams, bird omens, curses, evil spirits, and the realms of the dead. They were testing to see if God's Word addressed every issue. If it didn't they wouldn't dare risk trusting it; they'd be better off sticking with the spirits they knew.

So they took each subject and poked it with a stick. If we poke it here, what answer do we get? If we poke it there, is there a different answer? Does the same truth prevail in every situation? They asked the same questions of everyone who came to visit. And I'd think, *But I already answered that.*

People even came from other villages to ask questions. At first I didn't understand that this was the method by which societies with oral traditions validate what they hear. They ask their questions over and over again, weighing one answer against another. I'd get impatient when someone would just ask questions and not come to a commitment to follow God. But Ama would always tell me not to worry. "Don't you see, my child, they're starting, they're in the process of believing—they're asking questions."

As I struggled to explain things from the Scriptures, I learned a lot about the nuances of the language. People would lean forward, frowning in concentration, groping to understand what I was saying. Then someone would finally cry out, "Oh, I think I know what she means...." and I'd whip out my pencil and write down another treasure for the translation desk.

And in this long, repetitive process, people believed. Right in the middle of the meetings, people sometimes asked, "What is it that you say to God when you want to become one of his children?"

One man bowed his head and prayed on the spot. Looking up, he asked, "Is it OK if we tell this to other people? Maybe then the spirits will go over the mountains to Ifugao Province and leave us alone."

In those early years of Sunday meetings, my "little brother" Doming, then twenty years old, always came home on weekends from the town of Natunin where he lived and attended the only high school in Balangao. He came to the studies, but he questioned some of what was taught. He used to love to throw out comments to annoy me: "My teacher says the books of Moses are fiction." He was always baiting me. I used to ask him, "Why don't you be wise like our father?" But, like many twenty-year-olds, he didn't think our father was so wise.

Every Sunday fifty to sixty people would cram into my fourteen- by sixteen-foot house, and sit on the floor. They listened; they asked about God; they said they wanted to believe. But in spite of all this, my frustrations were mounting: the intensity of the spiritual battle had heightened. Every time someone tried to believe, the spirits would hound them until they sacrificed. People would get sick, crops would fail, and some people died. After one man started believing, his wife was diagnosed with terminal cancer. The Balangaos, both believers and unbelievers, understood this was the evil spirits retaliating for their loss of power and control. It kept some from believing and it deeply troubled me.

All I could do was pray and keep translating. I figured a newly born church could use the letters the apostle Paul wrote to Timothy and Titus. Tekla helped me. She never tired of working on God's Word, and she taught me about questions. "You jump too fast to answer questions," she admonished me. "Don't be so anxious; let them finish what they're asking before you answer them." And she taught me to ask, "What do you suppose the Bible means when it says?...." and, "Why do you think God says that?" My answers were well received when cloaked in questions.

More and more people believed and as the months went by, I became increasingly uncomfortable being their only teacher. I suggested that I go over the Scriptures with them on Saturday and then they could teach on Sunday. I could help them answer people's questions. But they refused. I argued, I begged, I reasoned, but they would not teach. "We don't know enough to teach," was their excuse.

Then one day I was checking 1 Timothy with Ama. We came to 1 Timothy 2:12 where Paul says to Timothy, "I do not permit a woman to teach...a man." Ama never said a word; we just went on checking. But late that afternoon, when we were finished for the day, he asked me what we were going to study on Sunday. Assuming he was just curious, I was delighted to tell him. Then on Sunday morning, after the singing finished and before I could stand up, Ama rose and, nodding toward me, said, "My daughter here knows more about this than I do, but we found in the Bible where it says that women aren't supposed to teach men, so I guess I have to be the one."

My Balangao teaching career was over. Ama led the Balangaos into church leadership.

As teachers, the Balangao people were experts in eliciting questions, and patient about answering them. Now the experts were the teachers in the church.

But still the spirits harassed the believers.

At the translation desk, my mind would fly away from the Scripture portion at hand and my heart would cry, "God, can't you do something? You've got to defeat these spirits."

I'd wake up at night and plead with God, "God, *do* something—show these Balangaos you are powerful; defeat the spirits."

13
This Is War!

Tekla and I were working extra long hours as we tried to get the book of Titus translated for the coming workshop in Bababag. Suddenly a neighbor burst in the doorway shouting, "Come quick! Benito's son is dying!"

Benito had just become a believer. Earlier in the week his aunt had almost died and just yesterday his daughter had almost bled to death in childbirth. I called, "Bring the boy up here, this is the house where the medicine is." They left, but no one came back.

Tekla ran to see what had happened and a few minutes I heard her scream for me to come. I raced down stone steps and through stone-paved yards to Benito's house and scrambled up the ladder.

I saw it all in a glance: the house packed with people, the boy writhing in convulsions in one corner, and his near-hysterical mother screaming at the spirits, begging them to accept something in place of the child's life. "We have four pigs! We have ten chickens! We have rice! What do you want? What do you want?" Benito wasn't even there—he was off in the forest getting firewood.

The spirit medium, old Chalinggay, crouched in the center of the room, holding her beads and shaking uncontrollably as the spirits moved into her body. The spirits were obviously speaking—the voice was not Chalinggay's.

Anger welled up in me. I was so furious at what the spirits were doing that I forgot my fears. Every time someone wanted to believe, those spirits would raise havoc. Without thinking, I shouted at Chalinggay, "Get out!"

And all the people yelled back, "No, wait, the spirits haven't said what they want yet!!"

I yelled at her again, "Get out—leave!"

The people screamed back at me again, "Wait!"

In frustration I gripped the old woman's shoulders and pushed her over to the door and resolutely down the ladder. I took a deep breath, then turned to explain to the stiff and silent crowd, "I'd never do anything like this under different circumstances; the spirits are doing this to Arsenio because Benito said he wanted to follow God. The spirits are trying to make him sacrifice. They're just trying to scare him. You watch, that boy won't die. You'll see that God is stronger than the spirits. He'll keep him alive!"

Faces had gone pale. Even Tekla was shaken. I nudged her and we gathered up Arsenio and carried him through the village to my house. On the way I silently prayed, "Oh God, prove yourself stronger than the spirits."

We lay Arsenio down on my floor and prayed; the convulsions stopped. We examined him: nothing was wrong with him except that his neck hurt. "Why does your neck hurt?" I asked.

"Because," explained the six-year-old, "when I saw the spirits coming for me, I tried to run, but they struck my neck with their machetes and I screamed and fell on the floor."

Arsenio was always throwing tantrums and disobeying his parents. We prayed over him again and then Tekla scolded him soundly, telling him that he'd better stop acting like a child of the devil, or else the spirits really would come and get him. When his mother came to take him home, we prayed with them again. "Don't be afraid," I told her. "Just watch and see how God will keep your boy alive."

Tekla insisted that we go to Arsenio's house and pray for him first thing every morning. She was still tense about my encounter with Chalinggay. And I had heard how offended Chalinggay was that I'd forced her out of the house.

Years later I learned what my real offense had been: you never interrupt a spirit while it is talking through a medium. If you do, the spirit will kill the medium. I had inadvertently doomed Chalinggay to death. People huddled in houses talking about how much they would fine Telka and me for murder when the medium died.

Though I didn't know that, I did know how hurt Chalinggay was about my rudeness. A few days later, on Sunday afternoon, I went to apologize.

Poor, old, crippled-up Chalinggay was tormented by spirits that routinely kept her awake all night. She usually slept from daybreak to noon. Countless times I'd tried to tell her about the God of heaven, but she never could grasp anything I told her. I had finally dismissed her as too senile to understand. That day I only went over to say, "I'm sorry."

But when I saw that pitiful woman sitting there, I couldn't help myself. I said, "Oh, you poor wretched woman, to be at the mercy of those spirits. Look what they've done to you—all your children are dead, your husband is dead, you're lonely, the spirits frighten you all the time…a really fine lot those spirits give you for all your service to them." My words just tumbled out.

She stiffened; she'd never considered the spirits in this light. She interrupted me and argued in self-defense: "But they make me do it; they make me do what they say."

I sighed and answered, even though I knew she wouldn't comprehend: "You don't have to do what they tell you… you can just ask God to send them away and he will."

Lips tight and eyes narrowed, she asked, "What do you say to God to ask him to send the spirits away?"

That caught me off guard; "Uh…you say, 'Dear God, please send the spirits away, in Jesus' name.'" She actually started practicing those words, stumbling over the name "Jesus." I was dumbfounded.

I wandered back up through the village toward my house, deep in thought, *You don't suppose that old woman would try praying that, do you?*

Little old Forsan, eager for gossip and vitally aware of the village undercurrents I knew nothing about, snagged me as I walked past. She was a spirit medium, too, and very crippled. But she was also a fun eighty-year-old with tattoos all down her arms. How that woman loved to talk! She'd given me detailed rundowns on the spirits—and I'd given her detailed rundowns on God. And she had carefully explained to me how the spirits put the beaded bracelet on her arm, and that they'd kill her if she ever took it off.

The most curious person I've ever known, Forsan fired off question after question at me as I walked by: "Where have you been? Who have you been talking to? What have you been talking about? What have they been telling you? What have you been telling them?" I stopped, thought, and then decided, *Forsan, you're going to get the whole load this time.*

Everything I'd said to Chalinggay came out in a torrent to Forsan, "All your children are dead, your husbands have died, you're poor, wretched, miserable, crippled, and lacking in life's necessities—it's a fine lot the spirits give you. Why don't you just take that bracelet off?!"

She reeled, grabbed her bracelet, and said, "You know they'll kill me if I do." She pulled further away from me. Feeling ashamed, I apologized, "I'm too blunt...." I tried some more gentle explanations for a while to smooth out the situation and then went home.

The next day, after praying with Benito, Tekla and I went back to translating—at last. We prayed for a good week of translating; the past week we had gotten nothing done because of the spirits' attacks on Benito's family. We even closed the study door, which was very inhospitable—but it seemed like everything was conspiring to keep us from getting our translation done.

Suddenly, there was frantic knocking at the door. I opened it; there was Chalinggay, wide-eyed and shouting, "Send them away! They're pinching me and kicking me! All night long I've been praying that prayer you told me, and now they're kicking me and pinching me—send them away!"

I froze. *What have I gotten this woman into? Now what do I do?*

Tekla pulled her inside. I prayed, "God, protect us from the power of the evil one. Send these spirits away...." Chalinggay traced my prayer, shouting every word after me. Calmness came over all of us. We prayed again, and after a while Chalinggay hobbled home.

I looked at Tekla. Tekla looked at me. I was wondering, *What are we doing meddling with the spirits?!* She wasn't wondering, she knew: This is war.

That afternoon a great, black thundercloud darkened our world earlier than usual. It was 5:00 P.M. and we were ready to quit work when the door flew open and Chalinggay burst in, running as best as a crippled old woman can. Sweating profusely, her face twisted in pain, she was bent over and clutching her stomach as if she were being stabbed repeatedly. Her body was going stiff in the jerky shakes that accompany spirit possession. "They're killing me, they're killing me!" She screamed. "Send them away, they're killing me!"

I was paralyzed with fear. *What have I done? Oh God, now what do I do?* I started to pray. Chalinggay prayed each word, right on top of mine. Then I stopped in mid-sentence.

"Chalinggay, the trouble with you is, you're not God's child. If you would repent of your sins, and ask God to make you his child, then God could protect you." I knew God *had* to help us in this battle.

Chalinggay didn't wait for me to pray this time; she just threw her head back and shouted up at God, "God, it is true, I am wicked." She looked down and muttered curses at the spirits, threw her head back and continued, "But even though I'm old, just a remnant of me left, make me yours and nobody else's but yours alone."

Instantly the shaking stopped and the pain vanished: the spirits had fled. Wonder and awe filled us all. Fifteen minutes later Chalinggay was slapping her leg and laughing out loud at the news that the angels in heaven were playing gongs and dancing, rejoicing because she had become a child of God.

Then I surprised even myself. "Let's prove God's power and ask him to give you a good night's sleep," I ventured. This seemed an easy enough prayer after the last one. We prayed together again, and she left.

First thing next morning I raced down to Chalinggay's house to see if she'd slept, if the spirits had bothered her.

She was ecstatic. She told me she'd slept all night long. "When the spirits would come, I'd just ask God to send them away and he would, and I'd go right back to sleep."

I was awed at what God had done. With those problems resolved, I was able to turn my mind to work as I walked home. I thought, *Now, at last, today we are finally going to be able to get some translation done.*

Two hours later, as we were back at the desk, poring over verses, Tekla and I were interrupted again by a knock at the closed door. There stood frail, bent-over Soya-aw, Forsan's husband, calling us to come: "Forsan is dying."

Emotionally, I was depleted. My work weighed heavy and I could only sigh. Forsan was so old, and often the old ones hovered for days between life and death. If I stayed at her deathbed I'd lose even more translation time. But I never could resist the old ones, especially funny, curious Forsan. I sighed and optimistically left my exegetical helps open on the desk. Then Tekla and I trudged down to Forsan's little house, and climbed up the rickety ladder. The floorboards were rotting, the roof was leaking, and Soya-aw was right: Forsan was dying. But I couldn't figure out why. *What is wrong with this old woman?*

Usually I could suggest some kind of remedy, but this time I was stymied. I said, "Forsan, if only you could trust God, he could help you, but I just don't know what to do."

Then Forsan held up a skinny, wrinkled, bare arm. The spirit bracelet was gone.

"I am trusting God," she said. "That's what's wrong!"

14
Victory

———⟨⟨⟩⟩———

Panic flooded me. Forsan was dying. She had defied the spirits and now they were killing her. My thoughts raced. *What have I gotten her into? Now what do I do? What did we do yesterday with Chalinggay?* Then I remembered that Chalinggay was released from the spirits when she prayed and acknowledged her need for God. I led Forsan in a prayer, modeled after Chalinggay's of the day before. Forsan, too, became a child of God.

Though the spirits no longer harmed her, Forsan didn't respond immediately like Chalinggay had. It took several days for her to recover completely. Tekla was eager to make the rounds each day with me and pray for Arsenio, Chalinggay, and Forsan—she knew the village unrest and that disrupting spiritual powers meant virtual warfare.

All this was teaching me that God works differently with each person who turns to him. Some experienced immediate and dramatic freedom from the spirits; for others it took time. But the power was always from God, and it was always his choice how he handled it.

When I went to pray with Forsan one morning, she told me the spirits had come in the night and tried to lure her with a beautiful new dress, but she wouldn't take it. "No," she told them, "God would be angry."

I counseled her to continue obeying only Jesus Christ. "Forsan," I told her, "if those spirits say, 'Stand up,' you sit down; if they say 'eat,' don't eat. Don't obey anything they tell you, just obey God."

For many years Forsan had ridiculed Tekla because she refused to sacrifice. But as soon as Forsan believed, she called Tekla for help. Forsan begged Tekla's forgiveness and then asked her what to do about her backpack of spirit paraphernalia. Immediately Tekla helped her burn some of it, and together they defiled* what they couldn't burn. The people were terrified.

The news spread and in a couple of days the whole village was crowded with people from all over. They tried to explain to me, "You don't understand...you're a foreigner. Those women can't do that, the spirits will kill them...they just can't do that—you don't understand." They explained that in the past those who had tried to quit serving the spirits had

---

*The Balangaos defiled spirit paraphernalia by using it in a mundane way such as eating off the dishes that were reserved for spirits only.

paid with their lives. Now people were literally standing around watching, waiting for the two women to die.

But nothing happened. By Sunday it was obvious to the Balangaos that the spirits couldn't kill the women. That morning the Sunday Bible study exploded from sixty people to over two hundred people. We took all the furniture out of the house and people sat shoulder to shoulder on the floor, filling the house. People were standing on the porch and in the doorways and peeking through the windows—even the yard was full. The atmosphere was electric. I was riddled with questions the entire morning. They all wanted to know, "Who is this God that has more power than the spirits?"

After that the crowd never did thin out.

Several weeks later, I was in Bagabag and Doming came to see me over a school break. He'd been away at college in Bayombong and had developed a façade of sophistication. He was telling me some of the many things he was learning and mentioned that he no longer believed those "Balangao superstitions" about evil spirits.

Later in our conversation I began relating what had happened with Forsan and Chalinggay. As I talked, Doming's eyes grew wide. Just when I got to the climax of God against spirits, I stopped. Doming hoarsely whispered, "Well…what did the spirits do then?"

I couldn't resist teasing him. "Oops," I said, "but those spirits are just superstitions and not real...."

Sheepishly, Doming dropped his learned sophistication and conceded to handle truth head-on: "OK, OK—just tell me what happened to the spirits."

Soya-aw, Forsan's ancient, withered husband, watched Forsan very carefully. After about two weeks he was fully persuaded that the spirits were simply not going to be able to kill his wife: this God does have more power than the spirits. Soya-aw set out to look for Ama, and found him bathing in the river.

Perching on a rock near Ama, Soya-aw cut the traditional small talk short and said, "Canao, you know God better than I do; would you ask him if he'd list my name in his book, too?" Ama prayed with old Soya-aw and God listed Soya-aw's name, another Balangao in his kingdom. Then Soya-aw started calling us to pray for him when he had an attack of his recurring abdominal pain—prayer was the only thing that brought him relief. In fact, he'd scold us soundly if we didn't get to his house quickly enough.

When we finished translating the book of James, I typed up a dozen copies to hand out to people who could read. I'd always disliked typing, but after seeing the power of the written Word, I couldn't wait to get to my typewriter and start typing. A man named Fanganan got one of the copies.

A few days later he came running, shouting, "Come quickly! Hurry...my boys are dying! They've been off in the forest and have eaten poison berries."

I was paralyzed. In all my seven years there I'd never treated poisoning. Finally, I stammered out, "But, but...I don't know what to do."

Anxious and frustrated, he blurted out, "Well, can't you at least come and pray? That's what this book of James that you gave me to read says you're supposed to do."

Gulp. I forced my feet to follow Fanganan home. Like James says, I prayed—though rather feebly. Immediately the boys' violent vomiting and diarrhea stopped. I was amazed. Fanganan wasn't. "That's what that Scripture says we're to do, isn't it?" He assumed God would be true to his own Word.

God wasn't finished surprising me.

Months later, when I'd just arrived back in Balangao after being away, everyone was catching up on all the news. We were an excited bunch crowded together on my floor. Choronag, one of the village ancients and one of the most powerful spirit mediums in Balangao, was sitting in a turquoise webbed lawn chair—one of our two seats which we reserved for the older, more respected people. He couldn't get a word in edgewise.

Finally, in a lull, he impatiently reached out and put his hand on my shoulder. I was surprised. In the Balangao culture men didn't touch women. "Are you done talking yet?" he asked. "Can you tell me how to become a child of God?"

"Oh, can I ever." So I did. This was unexpected joy. Finally we were ready to pray. I bowed my head, and was closing my eyes.

But this was Choronag's first time to pray and he didn't know that custom. He leaned back, looked up at God in heaven and began, "God, my name's Choronag, and I live here in Balangao...." For ten minutes he explained to God how he'd served the spirits and had lived contrary to God's laws, but now he would like to transfer his allegiance to him, the Creator and rightful owner of all men.

Most people made their decision to believe while in the company of others, often in someone's house talking late into the night. They needed someone who already was a friend of God to assure them that they, too, could actually be accepted by him. The elders constantly fulfilled that role.

Balangaos had always had village elders, older men informally chosen by group consensus to guide them. I usually sought these older people to work with me on translation; their status and their experience were invaluable. In the course of helping with the translation, they ended up with an unusually solid knowledge of the Word of God. They were naturals to become a new kind of elder, elders in the Balangao church. Early on they began teaching others what they'd learned about God from the Scriptures. The

Balangao Christians took God's Word and their newfound faith very seriously.

It was dealing with the evil spirits that I most disliked—I actually feared it. So, one of the first things I taught the elders was to cast out spirits. People were always coming to me to cast spirits out of a possessed relative or friend. Often I couldn't distinguish what was spirit possession and what was something else, but the Balangaos always knew. I didn't know much, but I told them the three things I did know to do: bring someone with you, check yourself for unconfessed sin so you are clean before God, and ask God to send the spirits away.

God defeated the spirits so dramatically and so often that we came to expect the miraculous. That's why I wasn't afraid when they came running to me with Baltazar's little boy who was unconscious.

The child had been with his granddaddy, who was a spirit medium. The old man was sacrificing a pig when this little boy, not quite six years old, cut off one of its ears and was playing with it. The spirits spoke through the grandfather: they wanted that ear back. But the boy wouldn't give it to them. So, the spirits said they'd just take the boy, and he fell over unconscious.

His parents were terrified; there was no sacrifice to atone for defying the spirits. They scooped him up and came running to my house.

I quickly sent for the elders and we did what we always did—we prayed. And prayed. And prayed. Finally they took him home. And then, clear across the village I heard it. That distinctive cry, clear and melancholy, rising and falling rhythmically in pitch and volume—the death wail. The boy had died!

No! No! My mind was screaming. *What has happened? What went wrong? Why did he die? This isn't working. God, you've made a mistake. Now people will just stop believing.*

I couldn't face any of the people in the village. I turned on the two-way radio and called my colleagues in Bagabag, "Someone's got to come here! I've got to talk to somebody!" Then I ran off to the airstrip, sobbing all the way. Soon after I arrived, Bob Griffin landed.

Between sobs I poured my pain out to him—the loss of all the Balangao to the Gospel. Bob listened until I had nothing left to say. He prayed with me. Then as he climbed back into the little plane, he said, "You wait here. I'll be right back." In an hour he returned with his wife Louise. "You need someone to spend the weekend with you," he said.

Believers surrounded Baltazar's grieving family day and night. The comfort and reality of God were irresistible. A week later the entire family of that little boy became believers. I was dumbfounded. Maybe like Andrea they felt that God had the right to handle things his own way. While they mourned their son, his death didn't change the fact that God was all powerful and to be obeyed.

I simply had to resign as the manager of God's glory.

15

Of Locusts and a Helicopter Crash

Starting in high school I prayed daily for the people I'd someday work with. And God answered: I arrived in Balangao and met Tekla, already longing to know God. I had diligently prayed that Balangaos would turn from the spirits and trust the God of heaven. God answered again: they started to believe. Then I'd begun waking up in the night, pleading with God to defeat the spirits. And God, who had awakened me to pray, answered my prayers.

Now, I was praying through the day and waking up at night again. "God, teach these new believers how to pray. How to really pray. Do something, Lord." They knew how to pray for birth into God's family. But they didn't understand about asking for God's help with the everyday issues of life. They liked it when I prayed, but they wouldn't pray.

111

They wouldn't even pray at mealtimes until Ama and I were translating the book of 1 Timothy. We got to chapter 2, verse 8: "I want men everywhere to lift up holy hands in prayer." That night at dinner as I was about to give thanks for the food, like I always did, Ama loudly cleared his throat and said, "I will be the one to pray tonight." And that marked the beginning of men praying at mealtimes. But they still didn't pray about other things. *Why can't they get the picture?* I wondered.

One day I heard that the locusts had come back to the mountains. The Balangaos told me how some thirty-five years before, the valley had been stripped of everything green by the locusts. When they'd descended into the valley, people had gone out into the fields screaming and shouting and beating gongs, but to no avail. They lost everything.

And now it had happened again: the locusts came in a black cloud. People ran to the fields and shouted and screamed and beat gongs. But this time the locusts left. The Balangaos were ecstatic. They'd frightened the locusts away. I closed my eyes and imagined all those Christians frantically beating their gongs and shouting instead of calling out to God. *Why couldn't they rely on God?*

Incredulous, I asked the believers, "Didn't anyone think to pray? Didn't you shout and scream and pound gongs thirty-five years ago but to no avail? Did *nobody* recognize this as God's protection from the locusts?" They were quiet.

I took a deep breath. *These Balangaos are too human. They run on their own strength, relying on the basic principles of the world.* I wondered what had to happen before they asked for God's help and would recognize his mercy when it came.

The believers were embarrassed—it just hadn't occurred to them that God had power over locusts. Those locusts were the last straw. The next time I woke up in the middle of the night, I prayed, "God, I don't care *what* you have to do, just make these people pray." And then I slept.

Dr. Robbie Lim was an answer to a different prayer of mine, a prayer for someone to lift my medical load. A Filipino doctor under the auspices of the Catholic Mission, he came to work with the Balangaos and was preparing to build a small hospital to serve all of the Balangao people. Already he's greatly reduced the number of medical emergencies I had to deal with.

I liked Robbie. He was special. Many of his peers had gone overseas for higher-paying jobs and an easier life. But he had a servant's heart; the mountains challenged him and the needs only sharpened his skill. He cared about people. Now our dream for a hospital was coming true.

The Jolly Green Giant helicopter and its American military crew were in the Philippines on a break from the war in Vietnam. Somehow Robbie's request to airlift building materials for a remote hospital reached them and they jumped at the chance to help. All of my colleagues in Bagabag were caught up in the excitement as tons of cement and building materials were loaded into that helicopter.

I was to go along as interpreter for the pilots. Doming was returning to Balangao for summer vacation and we offered him a free ride home. A pilot, Bill Powell, who had often flown into Balangao, came along to guide the pilots into the area.

My parents had come from California to visit me. As we watched the men load the helicopter I would be flying in, Dad kept mumbling, "They're overloading that thing." He had an uncanny eye for weight and volume. But Robbie was thrilled; overload was impossible for this kind of machine, he'd been told. Later I learned that Dad could hardly restrain himself from pulling me off that helicopter when it lifted off. But we did take off, excited beyond words—a hospital at last! And then, thirty minutes later, we hit that betel nut tree.

The tree threw the rotor out of balance and we went down quickly in a deep ravine. The ship was thrown over but the rotor kept thrashing, shaking the helicopter violently. Cement powder flew in all directions.

The tail section was on fire, but Bill thrust his arm through the cockpit window and scrambled out of the wreckage. The pilot, co-pilot, and navigator behind him were all right. As Bill gathered his wits, he realized that three people were still trapped inside under tons of building materials: me, Doming, and Dr. Lim. Although he was sure we were dead, he ran back down the bank to get us.

But his left arm was useless and he couldn't pull himself up inside the aircraft. He saw fuel gushing out from a hole in the belly of the helicopter. "Juami, Doming, and Dr. Lim are inside," he shouted to the Balangaos who had gathered. Immediately they formed a bucket brigade, dousing the fire with water and mud. Others jumped up on the craft, climbed inside, and started throwing kegs of nails and bags of cement out of the craft until they heard my feeble cry and were able to dig us out.

The Balangaos stayed close by me all through that night...praying, "God, don't let her die—the Book's not done yet."

The next day I was airlifted to a United States Air Force base where young medics worked over me, teased me about how good-looking I was, and asked me for a date.

When they told me my mom was on her way to be with me, I couldn't wait for her to arrive. Mom was a nurse and had twenty years of experience with trauma cases. But when Mom walked in and saw me, she screamed. That's when I realized I was badly hurt. The nurses wanted to shave my head, but Mom wouldn't let them. She spent the day gently removing the blood-caked cement out of my hair and then washing my hair.

The first four days I reasoned with God that I couldn't go blind. I wasn't finished with what he'd sent me to do. When I was able to open my eyes a crack, I could distinguish light, then shapes appeared. What a relief! I could finish the translation.

The second week I was transferred to Manila. The damaged nerves in my right arm and side began to awaken, no longer numb. The pain was intense. That pain was almost my defeat as the doctors wouldn't give me any painkillers for fear I might get addicted to them. I thought patients in hospitals were supposed to be close to God—I was just in pain. I couldn't see God anywhere. I couldn't feel him, I couldn't hear him; there were no waves of glory, just wave after wave of pain.

Many pain-filled nights I couldn't sleep. Mom stayed awake with me most of those nights, holding my hand, only snatching a little sleep on the narrow cot beside me. I couldn't stop myself from thinking about Robbie's death. He'd been so excited about the hospital. All his efforts were being realized. I wondered if some people were wishing I had died instead of Robbie.

Weeks later, when I had healed enough to leave the hospital, Mom flew home to California. I made a quick visit back to Balangao—just for a day—to prove to them that I really was alive. Doming had changed. While buried under all that cargo, he'd prayed, "OK, God, if you let me live through this, I'll serve just you. I'll give you my whole life."

I had seen glimpses of our father Ama's character in Doming. So when he said he had given his life to God in the helicopter, I knew he meant it.

After six more weeks of resting and mending, I returned to Balangao to carry on with the translation. I was astounded to find Balangaos still praying. At last they had learned that they could pray about everything, big or small. Fervent prayer had become a part of their lives. They've never been the same since the helicopter crash. And neither have I.

16
Facing God

Forsan used to hobble over to my house and sit next to me and gossip and joke. One time she rubbed her watery eyes with the back of a knobby hand, reached over and tapped me on the hand and said, "I forgot again. What is the name of the one I'm obeying?" She'd boldly changed her allegiance from the spirits to the God of heaven, but she hadn't mastered his name yet.

Like all Balangaos who believed, she'd wrestled with whether God was more powerful that the spirits. She knew the power of the spirits, but this other God…It was a wild do-or-die leap of faith when she pulled that bracelet off. And God proved to her and to all of Balangao that he was more powerful than the spirits.

For Balangaos faith is a matter of obedience. The one you obey is your true master. You watch his eyes, you watch how he does things, and you shape your life to conform to his. For them, believing is not saying certain words or repeating a prayer. It's turning and pledging your loyalties to a new power and basing your life on it. Ama called it facing God.

Countless times God used a death to turn people's minds to eternal and spiritual things as believers explained about the God of heaven. When someone died, people came from far and wide and gathered at the house of the "dead one." Upon arrival, they climbed up into the house and squatted by the body, their head in their hands, and in a cathartic chant reserved for mourning, they wailed to the dead one their last words of grief or anger or even reprimand for leaving them.

When they finished, they dried their tears, sat with all the others, and talked through the night about endless unrelated topics in a futile attempt to distract attention from the death.

But when believers started attending these wakes, they brought something new into the scene: hope. They chanted and wailed, but then they deftly turned the conversation to new spiritual insights: resurrection and heaven. Because they spoke directly to the ache of the heart, the Christians were in demand when someone died.

"Come," the family of the dead one would plead, "and tell us about heaven and life after death." And as believers sat crammed inside houses huddling with mourners around a corpse, their witnessing had its most profound effect.

Ama also took advantage of other meetings to teach about the God of heaven. He took his shelf-paper genealogies everywhere: to school graduations, town meetings— any gathering. When it was his turn to speak, he unraveled the scroll, which captured the attention of the crowd, and he explained what was written there. People strained to see, and they listened, riveted to the spot. They talked and asked questions.

The Balangaos were learning to trust. Slowly they were coming to understand that God's Word would give them instructions on how to live. One time a group of elders had visited a church in another area which forbade its members to chew betel nut. They came back wondering if they should do the same.

Betel nut chewing is a custom that acts as a social glue among the mountain people. The exchange of the betel nuts, the lime, and the leaves necessary for chewing is a type of bonding that happens when Balangaos meet on the trail, when they sit around and talk at night, when they gather to settle cases, and always at celebrations.

Preparing the betel nut chew is part of their lives. Men and kids shinny up lanky betel nut palms to pick the mature nuts. Every few weeks the men make lime by burning neatly stacked pyramids of snail shells. They fan the fire to get it as hot as possible. It burns brilliantly until the snail shells are snow white, completely intact in the ashes. Everything but the lime has been burned. After the shells cool, the men pick them up and put them in the rice mortar. Then they sprinkle them with water, which generates sudden heat, and they can easily pulverize them. They store the powder in a section of bamboo stopped up with some leaves.

Men and women put the lime, some nuts, a certain kind of leaf, and a homemade knife in a pouch that hangs around their neck like a long necklace. They wear it every-where. When they meet someone on the trail or sit down to chat, out comes the pouch. One person passes around the nuts; another provides the leaves; they share the lime.

Then each one puts a portion of a nut on a green leaf, sprinkles it with lime, wraps the leaf around it, and pops the bulky wad into his mouth. He chews it well, and spits out a thick, blood-red substance. Those who chew a lot have red teeth.

Outside they spit the red stuff anywhere; inside the house, they aim expertly at cracks in the floor or an open window or door. And the pigs and dogs that sleep under the house are decorated in red. During my first few months in the village those red splotches startled me. I had to keep reminding myself they weren't blood.

When the Christians came to ask me what I thought about the church forbidding members from chewing, I sent them back to Scripture. "See what you can find about it in the Bible." They couldn't find anything.

"Is there anything about gossip in the Bible?" I asked. There was plenty.

Since that was a much bigger problem in Balangao than betel nut chewing, I suggested, "Maybe we should just work on what is clearly forbidden first, then we can go to the betel nut." They still haven't gotten to betel nut chewing.

The church continued to develop. When Fanganan went out to join the military, the application form required him to state his religion. He had to think about that one. When he came back later, he chided me. "You never told us what religion we are."

Curious, I asked him, "What did you write on the form, then?" He said the only answer he could come up with was "Bible Believer." And that's how the Balangao church came to call themselves Bible Believers.

I used to shudder when people with false teaching came through the Balangao area. I wanted to forbid their coming or at least expose them. Once when one such man came in, I tried to persuade Ama to stop him.

Ama took a deep breath, looked at me sadly, and shook his head. "My child," he said, "you just don't know how to discuss things with others." He was disappointed that I hadn't learned how to when I'd seen him do it so many times.

I was caught short. I knew he was right. Sighing, I said, "Well, you're my father. I guess you'd better teach me."

So he sat me down and explained to me step by step how to deal with conflict. "First of all, you must listen. Walk along with the other person on his trail and affirm every point you can, demonstrating to him that you understand him. Then, when he's no longer threatened, and he realizes you understand his argument, take him by the hand and lead him where you want him to go."

The Balangaos are geniuses when it comes to interpersonal relationships and they taught me some invaluable principles about working with people. I learned to ask for their advice on many things.

The believers knew more than I did about presenting the Gospel to Balangaos, but I knew more about Scripture than they did. And that posed a problem: how could I, a child, correct the errors of my mother and father, uncles and aunts?

Doming helped me. He reminded me to ask them questions such as, "But now what are we going to do? Look, this is what the Bible says. So now what should we do?"

After Dr. Lim's death, I was again swamped with medical work. And the believers were begging for more books to be translated. So I told them, "If I had people I could teach to type and to administer medicine, I could translate more. What shall I do?"

They said to train a group of Balangao young people for those kinds of work. So some learned to give injections and do medical work; others learned to type. They intercepted the people who came to the door and talked to them before they reached me. At coffee break I'd consult with them about any complicated problems.

It was a good system. We were getting God's Word translated. And the spin-off was just as good as the goal: the many people assisting me saw the translation as their project, not just mine. They owned it. We were translating their Book.

And they were reading the Word of God in church—sometimes with surprising results. One Sunday a woman attended the service for the first time. She enjoyed the singing, but as they read the Scriptures, she became increasingly agitated. Finally, teeth clenched, she got up and slipped out.

Later, while we were eating she stomped into Tony and Tekla's house, walked up to within inches of Tony and, in a fashion untypical of Balangaos, she accused him to his face.

"The nerve of you! You invite me to your meeting and what do you do? You tell that man up in front every sin I have committed, and he goes and announces it in public. And not only that, but he reads it from a book! I'll never come again."

People were offended by the Scriptures often enough that the elders made it a practice to announce before reading from the Word. "You're going to think we know something about you and we're exposing it. But, honestly, nobody's told us anything. This Book just uncovers hidden things. It's just the nature of the Book."

17
Changes

The Balangaos still say that the best thing the airplane ever brought us was not the salt, sugar, and kerosene we needed so badly, but our visitors. Masa-aw said, "Our faith wouldn't be so strong if it weren't for all the visitors you bring to share their testimonies with us."

One time some influential people from Manila came. We sat in a circle after we'd eaten our noon meal. It was awkward having sophisticated upper-class Filipinos on one side of me and Balangaos on the other. They were worlds apart.

Masa-aw made the first move. Welcoming each one, he told them what a privilege it was to have them in Balangao. Curiosity was consuming him, so next he said, "Let's each one tell his name, what he does, and if he believes yet. And if so, how did he come to believe? We Balangaos will start with our testimonies here and go around to you and end with the Balangaos on the other side of the room."

The Balangaos started first to put their guests at ease. I translated. When we got to our visitors from Manila, they shared eagerly about their lives. The atmosphere had been turned around.

To hear the same truths about Jesus Christ from people from all over the world validated those truths and greatly enlarged their faith. And meeting their Balangao brothers and sisters also increased the faith of our visitors.

"This Book isn't a fable," Ama exhorted the Balangaos after one visitor left. "This is *real*—I've just met a man who actually drank water from Jacob's Well in Israel."

The Word of God changes people. The more the Balangaos studied and learned, the more they changed. One of the most amazing changes I observed was in the Balangaos' relationships with their mortal enemies, the Ifugaos.

Several Balangao believers and I were at a month-long translation workshop in Bagabag. Also in attendance were Len and Doreen Newell, translators who worked with the Ifugaos, and they brought with them their language helpers. The Balangaos and I invited the Ifugaos and the Newells to fly to Balangao with us for the weekend. Despite the fact that they had been hostile toward each other since their headhunting days, the Ifugaos knew it was safe to venture into Balangao territory in the company of their translators.

That Sunday we met all day long to study God's Word and sing. The Ifugaos were amazed at the number of

Balangaos who gathered to study the translated Scriptures. Even though a number of these aggressive Ifugaos had believed in God as they assisted Len in the Bible translation process, it hadn't occurred to them to meet and study as a group in their village.

But seeing what was happening that weekend sparked ideas in the Ifugaos' minds—the very ideas the Newells were praying for. Maybe they, too, could meet, and as a group they could endure the ridicule that would inevitably come from refusing to obey the spirits.

Balangaos and Ifugaos talked late into the night about just that. To defy traditions with these new ideas would be to invite gossip and mockery—the most painful blows the mountain people know. But the Ifugaos decided they must take a stand; they would make themselves vulnerable to this gossip and criticism.

So they invited Balangao believers to come to Ifugao territory to publicly baptize the first believers in front of the rest of the Ifugaos who still sacrificed to the spirits. The presence of the Balangao believers would bring extra courage to the hearts of these first Ifugaos who were publicly turning away from sacrificing to the spirits.

Weeks later three planeloads of Balangaos flew to Bagabag, about fifteen people in all. From there we took jeeps to the end of the road and then we hiked over the last mountain to the village of Batad. The Ifugaos killed a pig in honor of the Balangaos. It was exciting to me, but only a headhunter surrounded by enemies in an area without a peace pact could fully appreciate the awe Ama felt.

Ama baptized the first Ifugao believers.

Later he sat among Ifugaos. They chewed betel nut together and shared meat. He shook his head in amazement. "This is utterly impossible," he said. "It's impossible that Balangaos should be eating with Ifugaos. This proves the power of God!" All of their history never had seen anything like this performed without sacrifices and ceremonies.

But the changes didn't stop there.

The book we had just translated was always God's tool to work incredible change in people's hearts. When we translated the Acts of the Apostles, it was natural for the Balangao church to reach out to their Judea—the other people in the mountains surrounding them. Besides, they'd already ventured into enemy territory with the Ifugaos and knew God was powerful enough to protect them even outside their valley.

Forsan and Chalinggay, escorted by Ama and some of the elders, limped over to the airstrip early one morning. We were going to fly over the mountains to another village where new believers were struggling with the power of evil spirits.

We climbed in the little plane, the pilot strapped us in, and we took off. Forsan clung to me, digging her fingernails into my arm. I don't think those curious eyes of hers blinked once as she stared out the window the whole trip. Chalinggay hid her face in my lap and never looked up until we landed.

We'd been invited by these believers and their translator to show them that spirit mediums could believe in God and even stop sacrificing—and live to tell about it. When we arrived in the village, a crowd surrounded us. The two old women were seated right in the middle of the yard where everyone could see them and touch them. Ama told the story of how Balangaos had found God to be stronger than the spirits. People questioned Chalinggay and Forsan. When we left, one of the spirit mediums said that since those women had turned to God and didn't die, he would believe someday, too.

Back in Balangao I was still teaching the men on Saturdays so they could teach on Sundays, but already the Balangao believers had found the elders more accessible for advice than I was. It was 1974. I'd been there twelve years. The church was exploding, the Holy Spirit was blowing like a mighty wind, and there was no way I could contain or direct God's working among the people.

The elders taught, preached, and evangelized. I sat in Ama's house in the evenings after dinner and heard the men talk about who had believed that day or week while I had been busy at the translation desk. Ina prayed every day for the Book to be done. But in the meantime, the Word of God was changing people. I was amazed. Planting the seed of God's Word inevitably brings a harvest of churches.

In order to speed up the translation I asked Doming to pray about staying home from college for a year to help me.

I really needed his help and he'd already proven himself good at roughing out first drafts of the translation.

"Quit college for a year to help you with the translation?" He was quiet for a long time. I knew he liked working on the Scriptures, but I also knew how rare a college education was for Balangaos and how much it meant to him to have the opportunity to go. Finally he said, "Is this what sacrifice means?" He stayed home to help me the next year.

Every day Doming and I worked side by side on translation, each of us at our own desk. He made drafts of the rest of the New Testament. And he still took every opportunity to joke like only he could.

When we were translating Revelation, I explained to him about Christians going to heaven when Jesus came for them. He immediately came back with, "Oh good. I'll just stay here; then when everyone else goes up to heaven, I'll get everything they've left behind." I thought he'd gone too far. He still remembers the look I gave him. Of course, that was exactly what he wanted; he threw back his head and roared with laughter.

Doming was my disciple. We spent hundreds of hours talking about the Word of God, grappling with it, not just rushing on to finish the translation. I loved that time with him and with the others who helped. I loved translating that life-changing Book, the Word of God.

As I was translating Paul's letter to the Ephesians, verse by verse, thought by thought, I was gripped by the power of the message. I could imagine the Balangaos' response when they heard of God's overwhelming love. I knew wonder would flood them if they understood how God looks at us. Ephesians would instruct them clearly how to live as Christians. I prayed and wondered, *How in the world will we get this into everyone's ears?*

A plan started to brew.

18
Is This a Taste of Heaven?

"We could feed them vegetables," I suggested.

"No, you don't understand," they countered, "we cannot do that. That wouldn't be good enough; it would be shameful. Besides, we won't even have any vegetables in April."

True, there were only a few vegetables in April. But that was the best month because their field work was done and they had extra time.

"What if we flew in vegetables from the Bagabag market?" I asked.

Silence. Which, being interpreted, meant no.

We were in the middle of days of discussion about whether or not we could hold a Bible conference in Botac.

A few weeks earlier I had been thinking, *Balangaos always respond to the visitors we bring in...a large group of Christians sharing spiritual truths always multiplies the impact of the teaching....* A Bible conference would do just that!

I was sure it was a good idea, but since it was a new concept for the Balangaos, I began telling stories about Bible conferences I'd attended. I wanted to instill a vision. I hinted, suggested, and, in the end, requested the elders to host a conference: "Let's invite people from other areas to come study God's Word with us." We needed to share the book of Ephesians.

They said no.

I couldn't understand. They'd always been so responsive. I talked. I reasoned. I even argued. Night after night. Why didn't they want to invite people in to share the Word of God?

Finally the truth came out. They had refused for one reason: when Balangaos have visitors, they must feed them well. They must feed them meat. But the Balangaos didn't have enough pigs and chickens to feed one hundred guests plus everyone else in the village for three days. It's not that they didn't want to—they simply didn't have the resources. And they were too embarrassed to invite people unless they could feed them meat.

Christianity was confronting Balangao culture. Their pride about being irreproachable hosts kept them from providing for the spiritual growth of their brothers and sisters. But I knew that no matter how strong a hold their values had over them, God could break through with principles bigger than their culture.

We kept talking. I kept explaining and offering suggestions. We reasoned back and forth, night after night. After nights of no consensus, Ama skillfully moved in. "Yes, it is our custom to feed guests meat. And it's true, it's shameful if we serve them anything less...." He talked about the problem and then presented a possibility: "But maybe it would be possible to order dried fish and that would be enough."

On he went, the master negotiator at work. The Balangaos reluctantly agreed they would do it.

My co-workers in Bagabag became part of the Balangao Bible Conference by providing vegetables and dried fish to feed our guests. My main job was arranging for an outside speaker; Doming would translate from English to Balangao.

When the day finally arrived, our little village had the air of a county fair. They'd assigned committees and organized everything. I never would have thought to have a go-to-the-forest-for-firewood committee, but they did. Those hosting guests went to the airstrip to welcome the guests and take them to their houses where they would eat and sleep.

Everyone was nervous. The hosting families were nervous; their guests spoke different languages and they weren't sure how to put them at ease. And they still wondered how their food would be accepted. And the guests were a bit anxious about visiting Balangao, too; everybody knew a headhunting story to verify their fears. And when the speaker got up and seemed virtually tongue-tied, I was nervous. By the end of the day he was still strangely paralyzed, and I was distraught. I wrung my hands. *This whole conference is going to be a failure!*

But that night, as I went from house to house, I saw something unexpected happening. Believers and their guests had somehow overcome their language barriers; some were sitting up late into the night, sharing about their faith. Others were singing through the night, copying each other's hymns and translating them on the spot into their own languages. All of them were telling of their struggles and advising each other and praying together for each other in different languages.

The next day Masa-aw came to me and said, "I've never felt joy like this in my whole life. Is this a taste of heaven?"

The speaker was no better the second day. But that night the people again stayed up talking, singing, and praying. Then I started to realize that the Lord had his own plans for this conference, and they were different from mine.

"You say you're looking for a miracle?" Ama asked the group. "You'd like to see God's power? Well, look at it. Those Antipolo men walked all the way here through enemy territory, safe and unafraid. That's a miracle. Here are people from Sagada, Batad, Hamal, Amganad...all of us together. When in history did this ever happen before? We've never met before except to roll heads. Brothers and sisters, you are witnesses—this is God."

We had conferences every year after that. And the high-light was always people getting to know each other and learning from one another. They said that the mark of a Christian is that he can so easily share deep things. My adopted Balangao mother, Ina, asked me once after a conference, "What do people talk about when they don't have God to talk about?" Even when the teaching was good, the fellowship was better.

People from all over the Philippines were sent to attend our conferences. Jakiryl and his wife, Filipinos from Jolo, one of the southernmost islands in the Philippines, told a story which reverberated throughout the conference.

Jakiryl related how his uncle, his father's own brother, had murdered his father because of his father's newfound faith. And Jakiryl was not revenging his father's death. Not only was he not revenging the death, he was actually helping finance his uncle's children through school.

The entire scenario was impossible for Balangaos to grasp. In the first place, no Balangao ever would hurt his brother; that was unthinkable. But here was a man whose uncle had killed his father. They said, "Is that what the Bible means when it says, 'Brother will rise up against brother'?" It was further proof that the Bible really is true.

It was just as amazing that a murder would go unrevenged. And then to help the descendants of the one who had killed your father? When that impossible thought began to sink in, they asked, "Is that what it means to love your enemies?" They'd never heard of such profound forgiveness.

The Balangaos' world was expanding through visitors such as Jakiryl. And the power of God was magnified as they saw what he did in the hearts of his children.

As a result of attending conferences in Balangao, believers from Mindanao, Palawan, and other places started having their own Bible conferences. Seeing what had happened in Balangao inspired a vision for what could happen in their own villages. So, while Balangaos were encouraged by the faith and example of brothers and sisters in Christ all over the Philippines, their own example infused others with courage.

More than ever, the Balangaos saw themselves as a real part of the larger body of Christ, and they keenly felt their responsibility for the rest of that body throughout the Philippines.

One day when I'd just returned from Bagabag, Ama and I were out in the yard chatting and I was sharing a piece of news I was sure would overflow his cup of joy: a new translator had just been assigned to the nearest language group across the mountains. They, too, would get the Scriptures in their language.

But Ama didn't respond; he didn't smile. He was silent, deep in thought.

Tears welled up in his eyes. Then he said, "When those translators are ready to go, you tell them we will come along with them and explain the Gospel to the people while they write the language. That way it won't take them nearly as long to believe as it took us."

19
A Gift from God

Thoughts of a partner had been on my mind for a long time, even though I'd said little about it. I needed someone to help with the work: four hands are better that two. Even though I loved the Balangaos, I longed to have someone who understood things about me that were foreign to them—someone to talk with at length about everything from God to linguistics, from good books to curtain colors. Someone who would care about the same things with the same intensity. My life was full of joy and meaning, and great fulfillment, but all that still didn't remove the longing for companionship.

As long as I was only dreaming about the ideal partner, I imagined someone who could play the guitar and sing. The

Balangaos would love that. But I didn't ask God for all that. Maybe I didn't think he could afford it—he'd already given me so much.

It was 1976. I'd been without a long-term partner since 1964. That summer I went to Australia to teach in the grammar classes in the Summer Institute of Linguistics. My Balangao friends didn't give their blessings to that trip. Tekla's husband, Tony, had finally come to believe in the power of God after many years of prayer. Now he told me, "If you'd quit throwing your arms around so many other jobs, maybe you could finish our Book."

Others scolded, "You only talk about someday teaching us to read. When will you do it?" And they wanted me to spend more time writing songs and music. Me? Tony had said my singing hurt his ears. And the medical work was never ending. They were getting impatient with me and asked, "So why are you running off to Australia?"

One of my students there was Robyn Terrey. When I met her I thought, *No. I couldn't ask God for a new partner now.* But, little by little, it sank in. God could afford to give me another partner and he was doing it. And what credentials she had! Robyn was training to teach reading, and she was a nurse and midwife. She also liked my favorite author; she liked the same colors I did; she felt intensely about the same things I did—and she loved music: she even played the guitar and sang.

By the time summer classes were over, Robyn had decided to come and live with us and take charge of teaching people to read.

I returned to Balangao while Robyn finished her training. When I told Ama he was getting another daughter, he grinned from ear to ear; the Balangaos were as excited about Robyn's coming as I was. And they were almost as impatient.

You know you're really family when people fuss at you. When I told them it would be a while before Robyn got to Balangao, one old woman who'd been after me for years to teach her to read said, "Humph, maybe I'll be blind by the time she gets here."

When Robyn arrived in Balangao, I'd been there fifteen years. My friendships were established, my policies formed, and my patterns set. I was full tilt into translation work so I didn't have much time to help her learn the Balangao language. But Robyn got to know the school teachers right away and launched into training lay teachers with her first few words of the language. We worked each night on the words she needed to know to present the lessons the next day. She took giant leaps forward and soon was speaking Balangao well.

When Robyn had been there just a few days, a neighbor went into a complicated labor: a breech baby. How Robyn got that child out amazed me. I had to give him mouth-to-mouth resuscitation to make him breath, but it was Robyn who got him out to the air. Andrea carefully watched it all. Then just days later she herself saved a baby's life following a complicated birth. She beamed as she reported, "I did just what I watched both of you do and it worked."

One Christmas day they carried in a woman from another village who'd been in labor for some days. With a start, I realized this was the same woman Anne and I had helped after her delivery during our first year in Balangao. This time the poor woman had been in labor for three days and was almost dead from exhaustion. Her pulse was twittery and the baby's heartbeat was almost gone. The mother had no more strength and nothing was working right; even her contractions had gone haywire.

In two hours Robyn delivered that baby. But once out, the baby wouldn't cry; Robyn was tired, so I took over. I worked on that limp baby who'd been pummeled almost to death during days of hard labor. He finally breathed, but it took twenty minutes before he gained any muscle tone. In two hours he was wiggling and very alive. That's when we decided Robyn would be the obstetrician and I'd be the pediatrician. We were a team.

It was that way with our linguistic work, too. I translated with a team of Balangao helpers; and Robyn, with another team, produced reading books and teacher training manuals, and she taught and supervised the teachers. Because she was there, I could put my head down and finish the Book. It took five more years.

20

Reaching Out to Judea

The whole village of Mallango gathered around us; hundreds of people were sitting on pig troughs, stumps, and spare lumber pulled out from under the houses. Everyone was curious, listening, wondering, "Who are these people who fly in airplanes?" Robyn and I had flown with the elders at the invitation of Bruce and Judith Grayden who had recently begun work in that area. Soon the Balangao elders were talking with the Mallango elders about their translators and their villages.

Very soon the conversation turned to spiritual things. Questions came. And they came again—the same questions everyone in those lush, rugged mountains asked every time.

"Where did people come from?"

"Where did sin come from?"

"Why wasn't Satan destroyed?"

And they listened to the same answers over and over again, nodding as those answers affirmed what they had just heard.

Ama pulled out his yellowed genealogy from Adam to Jesus, and told them how God had used each of the people listed. And he told them, "If this would keep going down, even our names would be on it." As the years went by, he went through three shelf-paper genealogies as he drew others into his own wonder at the ownership of God.

By late afternoon, although they'd covered every question numerous times, the same questions still kept coming around. Finally we told Ama, "You've answered those particular questions well enough. You don't have to answer them again."

Ama looked down, paused, and with courage, quietly said, "We will answer the questions as many times as they ask them."

The elders stayed up late inside people's houses drinking strong, sweet coffee. As our eyes drooped, they sent us off to bed, but they kept on through the night. Different ones snatched an hour of sleep here and there. They were building relationships. Talking with new friends and discussing new ideas were more important than sleep.

Despite the lively interest in the God of heaven and speculation about believing in him, when we left the Balangao elders doubted anybody actually had believed during our visit. But they were optimistic about God's power and they knew God answered prayer. When they returned home, they prayed for the Mallango people every day at every meal.

The next time the elders went to the Mallango area, there were a few believers. By their third trip, many Mallangos had believed, and the Balangao leaders helped these new believers construct a church building and choose their own elders.

Bible translators working in other languages also invited the Balangao elders to their villages to give a Filipino's view of why these translators had come. The Balangaos always received as much as they gave. The vision to get God's Word into all of God's world flamed up in all of us because of these missionary journeys.

Ama's teary-eyed wish to help other Bible translators was coming true as elders went on foot, by plane, and by helicopter to various places throughout the northern Philippines to present the Gospel. The food, the customs, and the responses of the groups were all different. But some things were the same: the Balangao Christians who went always suffered hardships and they always took risks.

They sacrificed material goods when they left work undone at home and in their fields. They sacrificed comfort to hike over the steep mountains and stay up day and night for days on end, just answering people's questions and sharing God's Word.

Sometimes they risked their lives traveling through areas where there was no peace pact. Being beheaded was a real possibility, so they held their breath until they'd eaten their first meal—that pledge of protection by their host. In other places known for poisoning enemies, they watched carefully as homemade rice wine was poured into tin cups. When the hosts drank first, they relaxed.

After Robyn came, Tony and Tekla began homesteading near the Ga'dang people in Butigui, two days away from the Balangao area. Tekla said developing that land was the hardest physical work she and Tony had ever done. They started absolutely from scratch: they wove their own baskets, made their own brooms, and built their own house.

And as they planted their gardens, they tried to plant a church. Though there were believers there already, most of the others were resistant to the Gospel. Tekla gathered Ga'dang women together and tried to teach them how to read their own language so they could read the Ga'dang Scriptures. Tony told people about the God of heaven and encouraged them to read the Ga'dang Scriptures.

When Tony and Tekla were back in Balangao two years later, Tony stood up at the Christmas celebration to report what God was doing where they now lived in Butigui.

He started to speak, choked up, and couldn't talk. "Let's sing a song first," he said.

After more futile attempts and a number of songs, Tekla finally stood up and spoke: "The reason he can't talk is that he's overwhelmed; he looks at you and he wants this to happen in Butigui. This church is packed and people are spilling out into the yard. Everyone is praising God and wants to learn about him. But for almost two years Tony has suffered hardships trying to evangelize the people in Butigui, and still they won't believe. He's done everything he knows how to do." The church fell silent, Tekla sat down, we all prayed, and the service went on.

That night the elders went to Tony's house and prayed with him. They counseled him to give the Ga'dangs a global picture, starting with creation, and let them ask questions all the way. They told him to explain the bad news before he told them the Good News. To tell them how Satan is God's enemy and how the Devil uses deception and lying to make people play into his hands. Once Ga'dang people comprehended the bad news, the Good News would be good indeed.

Tony and Tekla returned to Butigui where the proclamation of the Gospel was still met with resistance. But two things were different: Tony's new approach to presenting the Gospel was more effective and the whole church was behind them in prayer. It was unparalleled joy for the Balangao Christians when word came over the mountains, little by little, that more people in Butigui were believing in Jesus Christ.

Doming was invited to speak at the Ga'dang Bible Conference. I asked him what he was going to teach. With a slight edge of defensive logic, he said, "How can I know? I haven't heard what their problems are yet." He went days before the conference, sat with the Ga'dangs late into the night, listened to them talk, and then addressed their real problems.

Ama and others understood how important it was to have the Scriptures in their own language, and they were always helping translators and their assistants understand each other and work well together on that arduous task.

Once, at a workshop, Ama counseled some troubled translation assistants on how to handle their translators. He told them many things including, "When the translator is putting pressure on you to come up with some exact word or meaning, and he keeps asking and probing, and you are sweating and can hardly think anymore and you have lost track of what he's after, this is what you do: just tell him you have to urinate. Then go outside and walk around and let your head clear. I think my daughter wonders why it takes me so long."

Another time the elders and I were back in the Mallango area where translation work had just begun. Somehow kind, gentle Bruce Grayden had inadvertently offended his friend, his main language assistant. As a result, the man would have nothing to do with him. He wouldn't even come near him. Bruce was bewildered, trying to figure out what he'd done and how to atone for it. When we arrived, he took Ama aside and asked him for help.

Ama went to the language assistant's house where they shared betel nut and talked about many things. Finally, the subject came around to their "American"* translators, and Ama found out what had happened.

The man was angry, and, to all mountain men, the reason, as well as the solution, was obvious. Skilled in the delicate art of handling conflicts, he expected the same from Bruce. His conclusion was, "It is up to him to realize what he has done to me."

Ama sighed and shook his head; he wiped betel nut juice from his mouth with the back of his hand. "I have had much experience with my American daughter and I can tell you this: even if Mr. Bruce thinks for one hundred years, he will never figure it out. You've got to tell him." The man sputtered and resisted.

Ama nodded sympathetically and said, "But that's the only way. They just do not understand. I have to carefully explain many obvious things to my daughter. They just can't figure things out. They're like that, those Americans."

---

*Bruce is Australian, but to the Balangaos all white English speakers were Americans.

21
Pushing to Finish

R obyn and I were so busy translating and teaching that most of the time we didn't go on the missionary journeys with the Balangaos elders. But when they returned from a trip, we'd go to one of their houses and sit on the floor until late at night, arms around our legs, chins on our knees, enthralled with stories of what God was doing in people's hearts. Eyes glistening, they often ended their stories with, "That's God working. Mere man could never accomplish that."

One time the elders were invited to teach God's Word in Pasil, where translators had been trying for many years to interest the people in the God of heaven. Masa-aw knew it was important for Ama to be on that trip—he would be well respected for his age. And the Balangaos had invited two men from Mallango to come along and teach. They were passing on their missionary vision to the Mallango believers.

Because someone had died, the entire village was there. They gathered around the newcomers. It was only natural that the old, esteemed leader of the area should do the talking. He welcomed the visitors and quickly fed them to put them at ease. All through the day they recounted the peace pacts in the past: who administered them and the violations that had destroyed them. Detail followed detail for hours on end, but no Gospel.

Later in the day, the whole village ate pig together. Long banana-leaf troughs served as communal plates; forty to sixty people at a time squatted on either side of them. Men walked past with flat winnowing baskets piled with meat taken from boiling pots; they handed everyone a big hunk. Broth was served in a short section of bamboo—a disposable, biodegradable cup.

They had finished eating their third meal; it was evening and they were chewing betel nut. The bridges of understanding and unity had been built. The old man of Pasil said to Ama, "You of Balangao and we of Pasil, we ought to renew our peace pact with each other."

"Yes," Ama answered, "in fact, that's why we've come here, to renew the peace pact. But the peace pact we've brought involves not only you of Pasil and us of Balangao, this one also includes the God of heaven."

Questions erupted; interest was intense. All through the night and for the next two days and nights, the Balangao missionaries accomplished their goal. People wanted to know more about the God of heaven.

But not every missionary journey was successful. Once after the elders had visited a village at the invitation of a translator, I asked Ama how the trip went. He shook his head sadly, "We weren't able to talk to them about God... they wouldn't ask any questions."

When I looked puzzled, he explained, "You can't teach people something if they steadfastly refuse to ask questions. That's just a courteous way of rejecting God."

Ama often mentioned that time with sadness. We never understood what happened. But we did learn that there are no sure formulas for people coming to God. And because of that, we tried all the harder to be dependent on the Lord.

And then there were Henry and Tagillap. The people from Bunot, a village two days' walk from Botac, had written to the Balangao elders twice, and now this last letter was addressed to me, pleading for someone to come teach them about the God we Balangaos were following. That's when Henry and his wife, Tagillap, agreed to move to Bunot.

They prayed for a way to earn enough money to buy rice to eat so they could teach the people there. We offered to send them some rice in case things got tough, but they refused. "No, we'll just trust God for it, or others might feel they need payment before they step out their doors to explain the ways of God."

We were translating 1 Corinthians. Doming was roughing out the first draft and Masa-aw and I polished it. We finished 1 Corinthians just in time for Masa-aw to rush to the house of a dying believer and carefully explain from the last chapters about the resurrection of the dead.

The man died, and at his funeral the elders read 1 Corinthians 15 from their own carbon copies. It came out so clearly in the Balangao language: God has put an end to dying—man will never die again. And because death has lost its victory over man, people do not need to fear death.

When 1 and 2 Corinthians came back from the printer, all two hundred copies sold out in two weeks. Marunggay bought one of those copies. She was an older woman who'd never been to school, but after she became a Christian, she wanted to read God's Word for herself so she enrolled in Robyn's literacy classes.

Masa-aw was walking by Marunggay's house one day and heard her talking. She was giving someone some very sound advice. When he looked through the doorway to see what was happening, he was astounded to see Marunggay sitting there alone, reading from a book. It was 1 and 2 Corinthians which had just come off the press. She went on, clear and smooth, just as if she were talking to someone.

Masa-aw climbed up the ladder into her house. "Maybe you have memorized that," he suggested. He turned over some pages in her book. "Here, now try reading this."

And she did, as naturally as if she were talking to a friend. Masa-aw couldn't believe that an old woman like that could read. Moreover, Marunggay could understand the deep truths she was reading. That was another radical thought. Back then, old women were mentioned in the same breath as children: "Oh, make it simple so the old women and children can understand it."

Masa-aw began to realize that God's kingdom and his truths were for everyone. He loved to quote Matthew 11:25, "You have hidden these things from the wise and learned, and revealed them to little children." To him, Marunggay was living proof of this verse.

Earlier, when Masa-aw and I had been checking 1 and 2 Corinthians, he had stopped, teary-eyed, and said, "Oh, this book—this book. It's really getting to me…I think this one is stronger to me than all the others so far." I had to remind him that he said that about every New Testament book we translated.

We finished the translation in 1979. Now we had to start the painstaking work of revision. Each word had to be right—these were the words of God.

Revision is a huge, complex job of integrating all the separate books of the New Testament into one whole Book. It's keeping track of how names are spelled and how concepts are introduced; it's a massive job of logging key terms and phrases and being consistent with them. It's making sure that the words used are acceptable to all the people who speak that language. It's also refining the first books we translated—all to produce an understandable Book which will impact its readers.

Doming was able to understand the Word of God and then paint vivid, unforgettable word pictures of its truths. He was delighted to take an introductory linguistics course to sharpen his skills as a Bible translator. He seemed a natural to become a Bible translator. But over the years as we worked together, he'd heard me dream aloud about someone to teach the elders and that vision had grown in him, too. Doming's heart was in training elders.

Help in the revision process came through Doming, but not in the way I had anticipated, for it was Doming who had introduced me to Ignacio. Ignacio's father was dead and there was no one to finance him through college. So, on Doming's advice, I arranged for him to have a part-time job as a guard at our Manila offices and I helped him through school.

Once when I was in Manila I approached him at the guard house. I didn't really know him then; to me he was just a tall, handsome young Balangao man from the next village. But I knew he felt indebted to me for helping him and I knew he would appreciate the chance to help me in some way. So I held out a manuscript of a recent New Testament translation and asked him to please read it for style and smoothness. He took it eagerly, but I wasn't expecting much from him.

But Ignacio surprised me. He didn't casually read the manuscript when he had a few spare minutes in the guard house. No, he took it back to his hot, little room and by bare-bulb light, he pored over the text. First, he would read the passage to get a feel for it. Sometimes in the context, he would spot slight inconsistencies that made him expect different conclusions than the ones the passage presented. Then he studied and thought and wrote out his comments. I was amazed at his insights into how to create nuances of meaning. He was a natural at linguistics.

I gave him another manuscript. It was the same experience. I asked him if he might like to consider doing Bible translation as his life's work. "Oh, no," he said. "I don't feel called to work among people who are already Christianized." To him that's what I was doing—working in a nearby village with the church that had been there as long as he could remember, and translating for Christians. Bible translation didn't seem to him to be pioneering or exotic in any sense.

"What I really want to do," he said, "is to take God's Word to people who have never heard it before."

"And, uh, when you find these people who've never heard," I ventured, "what language will you teach them in?" He said he'd just learn their language and teach in that.

I said, "Well, if you want to really learn their language, and it's unwritten, there's a linguistics course here in the Philippines that would help you do a better job of it."

I could hardly keep the grin off my face when I gave him the application forms a few days later. I thought, *You just wait and see! You just think Bible translation isn't reaching the unreached with the Gospel.* I knew the excitement he was in for. I'd heard this story before. I'd lived this story.

When Ignacio came back from the linguistics courses, he was the one who couldn't get the smile off his face. Laughing, he told me now he understood what I'd been talking about. He wanted to be a Bible translator.

"I was born for this!" he said. "I've been like a rock in a river bed, looking for a place to belong. And now at last I've found my wall, the slot I was born to fill."

We aimed at finishing the revision of the Balangao New Testament in 1980, but were forced to push the date back to 1981.

Even with Robyn and with all the help from the Balangaos, I was still struggling to get in six hours a day at the translation desk—sometimes it was only four.

I succumbed to asking Ignacio to postpone his linguistic studies to come home to Balangao and help finish the revision. I could hardly bear the thought of his putting off what he had at last found to be his calling. But he assured me it was all God's work. "Besides," he said, "I don't like the pinch I feel from God when I do what I want most rather than what God wants most."

Pushing to Finish

In 1981, God's Spirit moved mightily among the people on Babuyan Claro, one of the northernmost islands in the Philippines. The translators, Rundell and Judi Maree, were about to leave for furlough. On their way out of the country, they sent an invitation to the Balangaos. They said the Babuyan believers wanted Balangao Christians to come and spend a week on Babuyan Island and share their faith.

So Masa-aw and Fanganan went to teach the men, and two women went to teach the women and children. Both of the women left fields and gardens that needed weeding and tending. One left her three small children including twins, Joanne and Robyn. The men left their firewood unchopped and other heavy work undone. But Masa-aw spoke for all of them when he said, "The joy of telling people about God's Word was so wonderful that nothing seemed like a sacrifice."

They flew almost two hours in one of our airplanes. Having lived in the mountains, most Balangaos had no concept of *ocean*. When Masa-aw saw it from the plane, he wondered, what kind of a rice field is that?

They marveled as they flew past a larger island and then landed on a very small one. Masa-aw said, "Look what God has done. He has skipped the big places and chosen this small place in which to be rooted. God loves us insignificant ones.... What a wonder God is!"

Seeing the ocean up close armed Masa-aw with hours of fascinating stories. One morning he found a rock which stuck up out of the waves. He waded out, climbed up on the rock and sat there studying the Scriptures.

"Suddenly," he told me later, "the water acted like it was alive and could think. In some mischievous plan it just ran up and slapped me in the face and soaked me."

Another time I heard him telling some enthralled listeners: "You can't even bathe in it," he explained. "You are salted when you finish."

Masa-aw said Romans 1:20 came alive to him: "For since the creation of the world God's invisible qualities—his eternal power and divine nature—have been clearly seen, being understood from what has been made, so that men are without excuse."

People came from all over the little island and camped by the shore for the week. Balangaos led the Bible studies that filled the mornings and spilled over into the afternoons. They taught in the trade language. When they got stuck and couldn't find the right word, everyone struggled together in the search to understand.

Seventy-six people were baptized at the end of the week. Most had believed through the testimony of one Babuyan man who had tested God and found him powerful to change his own heart.

Another old man said, "I left my rice crop standing in the field, ready to be harvested, to come hear this so I might have a crop in heaven." He was baptized that week.

"The joy on their faces could be seen all week long. Oh, how hungry they were for God's Word," Masa-aw said. "We wish we could keep going back up there to help them, but it's halfway around the world."

Meanwhile, back in Balangao we were finishing up the revision. On Sundays the believers carried their eight volumes of trial edition New Testament books to church. One barefoot man said he felt like a student going off to college.

Even though I was disappointed to miss out on these trips, I loved giving them what motivated them to act— the Word of God. I'd always longed to be part of something bigger than I was—and this was it.

I had to be content to listen to their stories when they returned home. After we'd spent the whole evening hearing their reports, these Balangao missionaries would give us the names of the people they'd met and tell us their responses: some were asking questions about God and some were already believing. Then we'd pray for them all.

Finally, on December 16, 1981, we finished revising the Balangao New Testament. Then we started the lengthy process of getting the Book printed and we set the dates for the dedication. At last it was really going to happen! The Book was going to be in Balangao.

22
At Last—the Book!

Dedication day!

We'd planned to celebrate Balangao style for two full days and nights. No holds barred—we'd give speeches, play gongs, dance, and eat lots of boiled pig.

Airplanes buzzed through the sky with load after load of visitors and vegetables: eighty-two "Americans" and fifty feed sacks full of vegetables. The foreign guests brought sleeping bags and, by Balangao standards, an amazing amount of baggage for one night. The Balangaos just smiled and carried it all, and from time to time they offered their guests a hand on the slippery parts of the trail. Hundreds of other people hiked in for the two-day celebration.

Visitors ate and slept on the floor in the home of the family assigned to take care of them.

The celebration centered under a canopy of coconut palm leaves, blankets, and tarps quilted together to shade the side of the mountain below the church. Hundreds of people sat on steps carved into the hillside. The microphone was up front in full view.

A short portion of the program was written out, but the rest was completely open-ended. Everyone was invited to talk; anyone who wanted to sing was urged to come up and sing. Women had written songs about the New Testament and about the celebration; some sang impromptu songs about the visitors. Each village planned their own special presentations, and every single visitor was publicly introduced at the ceremony, an absolute must for the proper Balangao hosts. Pilot "Mr. Bob" and Louise Griffin flew in from the States and were surrounded by Balangaos who would never forget their help during those earlier years.

Then the Books were handed out: the very first one went to Ama. "This is what we've been waiting for," he called out, as he held his copy high, his eyes brimming with tears. Each one who had helped in the translation process received their prized possession.

Streams of people told their stories and recounted their struggles. I heard things that I had never heard before. It was only then, when Tekla told her story, that I learned how we had endangered Chalinggay by interrupting the spirits that day in Benito's house. And until that day I had no idea that Tekla had been accused of meddling with the holy Scriptures and polluting them by putting them in Balangao. I'd never known about her fierce struggle with God as she ran up the mountain to find me.

So much had gone on during those twenty years that I'd never seen or known. Friends had hinted at some things, but often I had missed at least one subtle but essential link that would have helped me understand. That day many things were tied together for me. I realized afresh that the Book was only completed because of the grace and wisdom and power of the God of heaven.

Late in the afternoon, Masa-aw made his way through the crowd and stood in front. The tall grass rustled behind him and coconut fronds clicked softly as he grasped his new copy of the Book. Leaning into the microphone and surveying the crowd, Masa-aw began to reminisce, straight from his heart, without any notes.

His eloquent speech, a highlight of our happy celebration, was the perfect summary of the past twenty years.

"Long ago..." he began, tilting his head back and nodding, "I'll tell you how it was with all of us long ago when these Americans first came here."

"Long ago, I didn't have the slightest interest in God. Then Juami and Anni came." He paused, looked across the crowd, and grinned at me. "Our first reaction was, 'Look, it's true—people can actually be white...look how white they are!'"

The young girls giggled, covering their mouths with their hands. The old people laughed and said, "Yes, that's just how it was!" "That's right." "That's what I thought."

A woman shouted Masa-aw's words into the almost-deaf ear of her uncle, who, tired of sitting, was squatting comfortably beside her at the edge of the crowd. He nodded, chewed, and spat betel nut juice into the bushes.

"Now, they were always writing down words and taking pictures. So I wondered, *Is this really a kind of work?* I tried to understand it all, but finally I said, 'Why, of course, they're just looking for a better life. They're going to take those words and pictures to America, make them into movies, and get rich. They're just people like us: they want to get rich, too.' That's what I really thought back then.

"My ears were shut to why they'd really come. Oh, they tried to make me understand. They said, 'Even though that's how you feel, just talk to us, so we can have someone to talk to.' And because we constantly went off to visit at their house, we began to hear the Word of God."

Masa-aw continued, "We listened and listened to the Word of God. There was no place to hide from the Truth, because that Word of God they kept talking about, it continually came out at every point to haunt and confront me. I was stymied; there was no alternative. So I said, 'Take me, God, I'm yours.'"

The crowd leaned forward to catch every word as Masa-aw held the Book up again. "And now I've a word to say about our thanksgiving in celebration of this Book.

"We have many things to give thanks for regarding this Book. What are they? The first is for the patience and endurance of those who came here to make this Book speak our Balangao language. Think this through with me: We could liken it to an unborn child which a woman carries. You women have tasted the hardships of being pregnant, haven't you?

"No matter what you do or where you go, you take that unborn child with you. Even if it causes you pain, you still take it.

"And so, likewise, this translation, this Word of God, was like their unborn child. They took it with them all over the Philippines and even to the United States. And just as an unborn child presents many difficulties, so this work brought them many difficulties.

"And, gracious, *that* unborn child—how many years were they pregnant with it? For twenty years!"

The crowd exploded into laughter. Nothing could be worse than a twenty-year pregnancy or more wonderful than a newborn child. The analogy was perfect.

"It's only now, July 24, 1982, that this book has finally been born. Why has this taken so many years? It's because that Word of God says, 'Watch out; be careful so that this work of yours, this unborn child, won't come to a premature birth and die.'"

Andrea listened, sitting by herself. Her two little boys were running around with the rest of the kids. Melisa would have been a budding young woman this year, had she lived. Andrea knew a lot about delivering babies, and she, too, had helped me deliver this Book.

"And so they came here, and they were very careful in forming the Word of God into Balangao. Some have said, 'It's just ordinary people who've written that book—it's man-made.' But I watched Juami and her companions. They were so careful they didn't even blink when they typed the Word of God, that's how careful they were about it.

"As for me, I'd sit by the hour, comparing references with them so the Book wouldn't have any errors in it."

Masa-aw opened the Book and slowly leafed through it to the middle and held it up.

"So let's not think just ordinary people created this Book. It's the exact replica of the original. And now this Book is our Teacher. So let's get a copy of this Book, and let it continually advise us. Whatever it tells us to do, let's do that. Because if we elect to follow just ordinary people, we'll surely miss the mark."

I stood in awe remembering the questions I'd struggled with so long ago. *How can I be a missionary? How will I know when I'm done? What could I do that would last forever? What if all anyone ever knew about God was what I taught them?*

Masa-aw continued, "Even though we don't understand other languages, at last a Book has been born that we can understand. Even though we aren't worldly wise, even though we haven't gone to school, even though we just cook our meals over an open fire in our house, we can still understand this Word of God—because it has come out in our language—Balangao.

"But what makes us most thankful of all is that people are believing this Book. Nothing else matters. Therefore, even though we're lowly people who just tie knots in our G-strings when we get up in the morning, what we teach is still very important. And though we've never gone to school, this is even greater than graduating from college; it is the most magnificent of all. For twenty years we've been studying this Word of God with nothing added to it to dilute it.

"Some people say 'Yeah, but when Juami leaves, it'll be all over.' That's what they say. And, of course, that would be true if we were following just people. But if it's this Book we follow, that won't happen. It will be our reference point.

"True, it's hard when our friends leave. Every one of us feels lonely when a friend goes away. Even the disciples of Jesus were sad when Jesus left. But Jesus said to them, 'It really is better for you if I leave. Because the one I'm sending to replace me, he is the Spirit of God who will reveal all things to you.' That's what happened when Jesus left and went to heaven and sent his Spirit."

I blinked back tears.

"And now it's his same Spirit who is in each of us, ruling over us. He is the one who works in us, making us steadfast in our faith. It's not a person that we follow. Therefore our faith will not fade away; it'll stand true."

It was God's Word in their own language that had called Balangaos to repentance, and his Word was still changing their lives. It was God's Word that the Balangaos needed, not me. And now, at last, they had the Book!

This day represented all that I had worked for, longed for, prayed for, and what I would gladly give another twenty years of my life for.

Only one thing marred my joy. I was going to have to say goodbye.

How can I ever say goodbye to my Balangao friends and family? Especially Ama—he's so old now.

And then relief flooded me: I wouldn't really be saying goodbye. I'd always go back to visit. Because that's the way it is with family. You always go home to visit, even if you don't live there anymore.

Epilogue

I 'll never forget Ama standing at the airstrip with me when I left Balangao after the dedication in 1982. He shook my hand for the longest time, his eyes full of tears, and he told me it was OK to go home. He knew how homesick my parents were for me and that I needed to visit them.

"Thank you, thank you," he said. "Thank you for coming. I never would have known about God if you hadn't come. And you tell your mother and father thank you for letting you come. And your church for sending you."

I choked back my tears. I didn't dare think about what this really meant, not right then. I couldn't handle it.

I climbed into our little airplane and flew out of Balangao on my way home for furlough.

A year later the phone call finally reached me. My co-workers at Bagabag had radioed Manila. Manila phoned the United States. A furloughing pilot traced my steps to a friend's house and she broke the news to me: Ama was dead.

I went numb. It felt like a light had gone out in my life. I had known Ama was old and ill; Doming had tried to warn me he might die. But I'd rejected the idea. The news stunned me. It was impossible for him to be dead.

Ama...the little man who marched into our house, told us we needed protection, and announced he would be our father. Ama, who'd always known just what to say and always said it so beautifully. Ama, who'd pulled me out of the pit of despair more than once. Ama, with a twinkle in his eye. Ama, who loved my cinnamon rolls. I loved him....

And he was gone.

A month later a detailed letter from Doming arrived, and I learned how Ama had died.

He and the family had been hours away from Balangao, working in his dry-land fields when he began feeling dizzy and an old ulcer started to bleed. By nightfall, the family knew it was serious and sat attentively with Ama through the night.

At 2:30 A.M. he asked them to prop him up. He sighed and said, "It's enough. You can take me now, Lord Jesus." And right then, just as the Lord Jesus took him, there was an earthquake, awakening all the Balangaos in their homes throughout the area. The Balangaos say the earth shook when Ama stepped into heaven.

They next day as they hiked with Ama's body back to his home in Balangao four hundred men lined the trail—a staggering number, even for Balangaos. For four days and nights, hundreds of people paved the entire village floor in Botac, showing their respect for Ama by staying with his body. Doming and the elders never closed their Bibles; day and night they told the multitudes the wonderful news about hope and a resurrection through belief in Jesus Christ.

Ama's death didn't end the Balangaos spreading the Good News in their own valley, throughout the mountains of northern Luzon, and beyond. Often at great risk the elders are continuing that work.

On one trip in the late 1980s, Masa-aw went with Ilat, an Ifugao evangelist, to teach the Word of God in Mallango. The two men were worried because they had to pass through an area notorious for civil unrest.

A few years earlier, one village had taken revenge on the Madokayan people by kidnapping one of their children and chopping him to pieces. As Ilat and Masa-aw got into the public transportation jeep, they realized everyone else was from the village of the killers. These traveling companions looked grim-faced and wore machetes, ready for action.

Ilat and Masa-aw got off the jeep to talk quietly together. "Is it safe to travel with them? Maybe we should go to Tokokan instead, and teach there. After all, they've been asking us to come." If they went to Tokokan, they would take a different jeep and travel through safer territory.

Then Masa-aw said, "But you know what happened to Jonah when he changed directions. He got swallowed by a big fish in the ocean. God said, 'Go to Ninevah.' Jonah didn't think that was a good idea, so he said, 'Well, I'll just go to a different place.' And look what happened to him."

They reminded each other of Matthew 10:28, "Do not be afraid of those who kill the body but cannot kill the soul." That settled it. They decided to pray and then proceed to Mallango.

They boarded the jeep again, started talking with one of the passengers, and found that he was from a place that had a peace pact with Balangao. And not only that, this man knew Masa-aw's older brother, the one who held the peace pact. Suddenly Masa-aw and Ilat weren't just unnamed faces; a relationship was uncovered and they were safe. But they had to risk the journey before they learned they were safe.

What about the other Balangaos? Ignacio has gone on to join the Translators' Association of the Philippines. His first assignment was to translate a few Old Testament portions into Balangao for experience before he moved on to a different language. In 1985 he and I reversed roles: he translated Proverbs, and I helped him check it. What a joy. I loved it.

A couple of years ago Ignacio was visiting in the village of Madokayan and asked an old man why they were so easily persuaded to follow false religious teachings. The man said, "Son, we've been waiting for ages for someone to come and really teach us God's Word. Do you blame us if we believe false teachers? I remember going to Balangao once during your Bible conference; you there have learned more and more about God because you have his Word in your language. But what about us? We have *nothing*. So, my son, don't ask me why—that's like putting the blame in us when we have no Book."

Ignacio almost wept. He knew then that God was calling him to translate the New Testament for these people who want it so badly. He and his wife and five children have just moved to Madokayan to start learning the language so they can begin translating.

My Balangao brother and co-translator, Doming, and his wife Loree have four children. He has an elders' training program for people from many of the mountain groups, and often teaches at the yearly Bible conferences. In addition, he's translating some of the Old Testament. After the Gulf War he began translating Isaiah so the Balangaos could stay informed about what is really happening in the Middle East.

Doming is over forty years old now, but he still loves to tease. He still cracks jokes, and I still wince sometimes— which delights him and the rest of my Balangao family. But when he preaches, my heart almost burst with thanks to God.

People lean into the wind, spell-bound by his exposition of the Word of God and his application of it to Balangao lives. He's a man with a heart for God, for his Word, and for people. Like his father, Ama, he's a man of integrity. When he sold out to God in the helicopter crash he meant it; he's honored his word.

Since my work in Balangao was completed, I've been in charge of the Anthropology Department of our group in the Philippines. I also help new members learn Philippine culture so they might serve Filipinos more effectively.

But I've got exciting news: our first printing of the Balangao New Testament is almost sold out. That means it's time to consider revising it and incorporating the translated portions of the Old Testament and then reprinting it.

How I'd love to go back and live in Balangao again and prepare for this second printing! Right now it's just a dream. I'll just wait and see what God wants…he has a way of transforming what I think are good plans.

And besides, I've never quite figured out just how to bring God glory. But I have learned to surrender my dreams to him. And he has made the reality of living according to his plan even better than my greatest dreams.